MACBETH
THE 1-HOUR GUIDEBOOK

AN ILLUSTRATED GUIDE FOR MASTERING
SHAKESPEARE'S DARKEST PLAY

David Grey & Gigi Bach, editors

SPARK PUBLISHING

Text and illustrations copyright © 2005 Bermond Press

All rights reserved. No part of this book, including illustrations, may be reproduced or transmitted in any form or by any means, electronic or mechanical, including photocopying, recording, or by any information storage and retrieval system, without prior permission in writing from the Publisher.

This edition published by Spark Publishing in agreement with Bermond Press.

SPARKNOTES is a registered trademark of SparkNotes LLC.

Spark Publishing
120 Fifth Avenue
New York, NY 10011

Printed in the United States of America

10 9 8 7 6 5 4 3 2 1

ISBN 1-4114-0448-3
Library of Congress Catalog-in-Publication Data available on request.

Cover and book design by Dreamedia, Inc.

LIMIT OF LIABILITY / DISCLAIMER OF WARRANTY: THE PUBLISHER AND AUTHOR HAVE USED THEIR BEST EFFORTS IN PREPARING THIS BOOK. THE PUBLISHER AND AUTHOR MAKE NO REPRESENTATIONS OR WARRANTIES WITH RESPECT TO THE ACCURACY OR COMPLETENESS OF THE CONTENTS OF THIS BOOK AND SPECIFICALLY DISCLAIM ANY IMPLIED WARRANTIES OF MERCHANTABILITY OR FITNESS FOR A PARTICULAR PURPOSE. THERE ARE NO WARRANTIES WHICH EXTEND BEYOND THE DESCRIPTIONS CONTAINED IN THIS PARAGRAPH. NO WARRANTY MAY BE CREATED OR EXTENDED BY SALES REPRESENTATIVES OR WRITTEN SALES MATERIALS. THE ACCURACY AND COMPLETENESS OF THE INFORMATION PROVIDED HEREIN AND THE OPINIONS STATED HEREIN ARE NOT GUARANTEED OR WARRANTED TO PRODUCE ANY PARTICULAR RESULTS, AND THE ADVICE AND STRATEGIES CONTAINED HEREIN MAY NOT BE SUITABLE FOR EVERY INDIVIDUAL. NEITHER THE PUBLISHER NOR AUTHOR SHALL BE LIABLE FOR ANY LOSS OF PROFIT OR ANY OTHER COMMERCIAL DAMAGES, INCLUDING BUT NOT LIMITED TO SPECIAL, INCIDENTAL, CONSEQUENTIAL, OR OTHER DAMAGES.

NEW & UPCOMING TITLES

IN THE 1-HOUR GUIDEBOOK SERIES

Hamlet
Romeo & Juliet
Julius Caesar
A Midsummer Night's Dream
Othello

CONTENTS

Foreword		ix
Character		
	Macbeth's Circle	12
	The Royal Family	22
	The Thanes	32
	The Minor Characters	42
Plot		64
Symbols & Themes		80
Scene By Scene		108
Appendices		
	Appendix A: Dramatic Maps	152
	Appendix B: Background	181

ACKNOWLEDGEMENTS

The editors would like to extend our warmest gratitude to the following people who supported us with their encouragement, feedback, proofreading and inspiration: Barbara, David and Beverly, Lisa, Brian, Professor Louis A. Montrose, Professor Emeritus Robert McCoy and Sterling Professor Harold Bloom.

FOREWORD

This book emerged from our desire to provide the unfamiliar reader with the most comprehensive, clear picture of Shakespeare's *Macbeth* in the least amount of time. In addition, our awe of Shakespeare's masterpiece nurtured a passion to present the information in a way that complemented the greatness of his work. Why shouldn't the beauty of a Shakespeare primer at least attempt to mirror the beauty of the subject? Briefly stated, why does a literary guidebook have to look ugly? The obvious answer is that it doesn't, especially when illustration collaborating with text is the best way to accomplish our desire for clarity and quick assimilation. Neither text nor graphics is exclusive to the brain. We think in pictures; we think in words. The cognitive interaction between the two is the quickest path to understanding.

When developing a picture of our audience, therefore, we held these characteristics foremost: frightening lack of time, need for clarity, desire for beauty.

Certain innovations arose in attempting to satisfy this model—visual distillations, plot timelines, dramatic maps, quick reviews of the characters, scene by scene illustrations and more. By the same criteria, certain traditional elements were eliminated—you won't, for example, find lengthy commentary in this book. Most of the commentary we have found in other study guides to Shakespeare was either overly obvious or arguably incorrect. To take up valuable time with our own commentary would be counter to our purpose, which we felt demanded concrete summary rather than questionable surmise.

As far as our specific decisions regarding *Macbeth*, at every opportunity we tried to convey some sense of the immediacy of the protagonist's situation—even switching to the second-person tense in our description of the hectic regicide ("How to murder a king"), complete with a diagram showing his frenetic path through an imagined castle floorplan. Time drives this play. We wished to communicate the feeling of the walls closing in we get every time we read this play or watch its performance.

We also tried to demonstrate the rich symbolic vocabulary imbued within this play. The language, though terse—like Macbeth's vanishing set of alternative futures—is remarkable in its sheer number of recurring motifs: sleep, babies, blood, natural rebellion, gender, clothing, darkness, equivocation, birds, illusions, Christianity and fate. The play is practically a kaleidoscopic recombination of these elements into one of the most code-rich, tersely poetic examples of dramatic literature. We found this quality so prevalent that we have included an entire chapter for its examination.

We adopted a convention of never referring to the Weird Sisters as witches. This was done for two reasons. First, they are never referred to as witches in the play, except in two unique situations: in the character direction for the actors ("First Witch") and in 1.3.6 when the first sister tells of the sailor's wife's insult, "Aroint thee, witch!" Second, we wished to emphasize the sisters' character of prescience ("weird" meant "prophetic," not "strange") so necessary to a reading of the play as a battle between fate and free will.

Our scene by scene summaries give equal, single-page weight to each scene division, except in the case of 1.6-7, 3.2-3, 3.5-6, 5.2-3 and 5.4-6, which we felt could best be dealt with in combination. After careful consideration, we also felt that the play should contain a final scene 5.7, rather than following the editorial convention of splitting it into 5.7 and 5.8. We ask your indulgence.

Congratulations on your adventure into Shakespeare's inimitable masterwork.

David Grey & Gigi Bach, editors

Dark, dark! The horror of darkness, like a shroud,
wraps me and bears me on through mist and cloud.
Sophocles
Oedipus Rex

Macbeth's *circle*

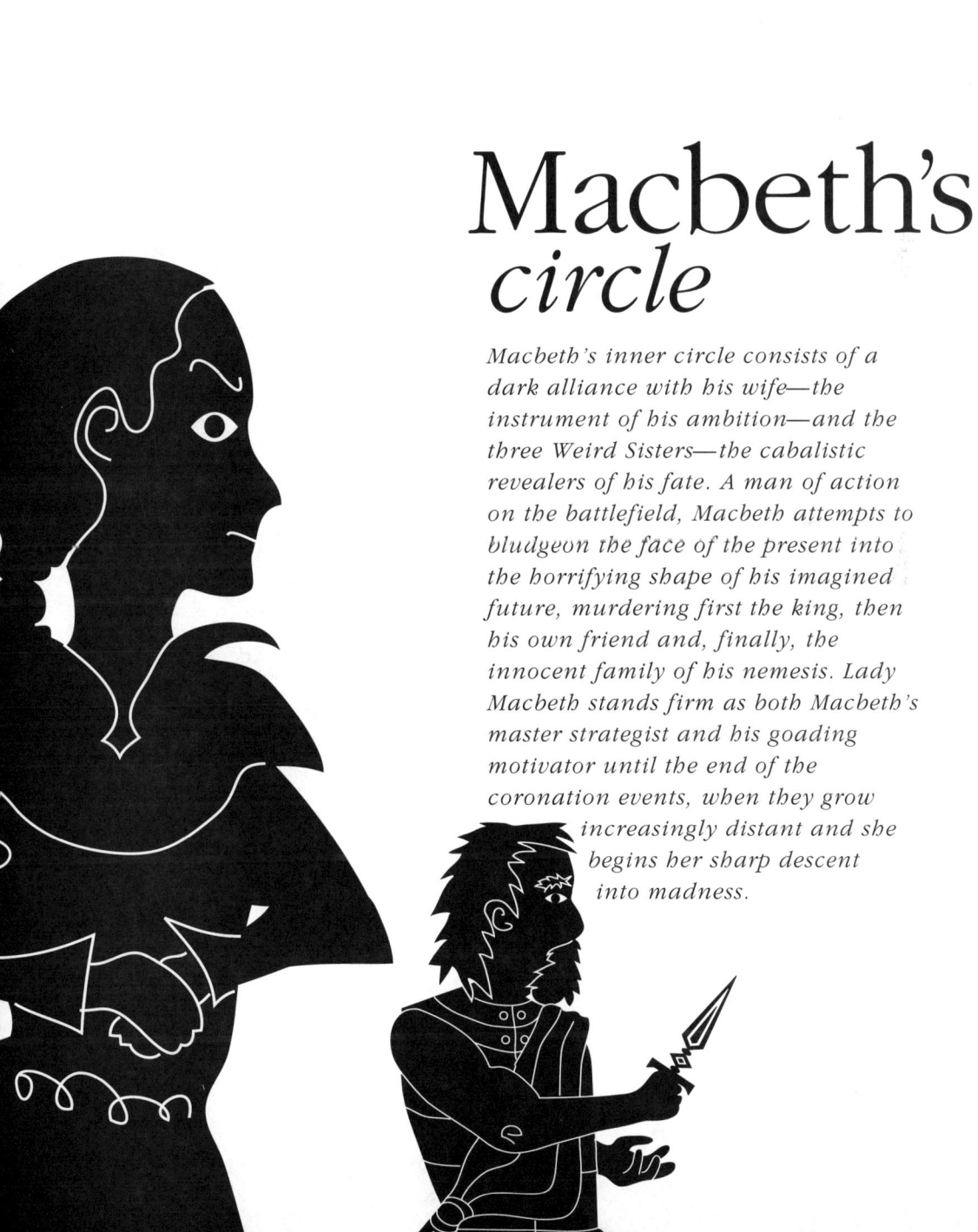

Macbeth's inner circle consists of a dark alliance with his wife—the instrument of his ambition—and the three Weird Sisters—the cabalistic revealers of his fate. A man of action on the battlefield, Macbeth attempts to bludgeon the face of the present into the horrifying shape of his imagined future, murdering first the king, then his own friend and, finally, the innocent family of his nemesis. Lady Macbeth stands firm as both Macbeth's master strategist and his goading motivator until the end of the coronation events, when they grow increasingly distant and she begins her sharp descent into madness.

PRESENT FEARS
*Are less than horrible imaginings.
My thought, whose murder yet is but fantastical,
Shakes so my single state of man that function
Is smother'd in surmise, and nothing is
But what is not.*

1.3.139-143

THIS IS MACBETH

MACBETH IS THE THANE (or baron) of Glamis, a township in the north of Scotland. He is, of course, the central character of this play, a dark examination of the forces of fate and free will.

Macbeth is a fierce soldier when we first see him—fighting valiantly for his king against both rebel and foreign power. When this violence serves the king, it is rewarded; later, when it serves Macbeth himself, it will be condemned.

I HAVE
DONE THE DEED

Macbeth receives a prophecy that he will be King of Scotland and, with his wife's prodding, he embarks on a mission to ensure its fulfillment by murdering the king. Once he is king, Macbeth begins a fruitless quest to exterminate all other predicted futures.

DAGGER
On the night he kills the king, Macbeth sees the image of a bloody dagger floating in front of him—which will be our shorthand symbol for Macbeth.

MORALITY
Though Macbeth is the tragic protagonist, which requires a degree of bonding from the audience, his actions in the play are abhorrent. Shakespeare saw no requirement for moral clarification, leaving his play open for greater possibility and interpretation.

BY THE PRICKING
of my thumbs,
Something wicked this way comes.
Open, locks,
Whoever knocks!

4.1.44-47

QUESTION
At the beginning of the play, Macbeth is thane of what township in Scotland? (ANSWER ON PAGE 18)

THESE ARE MACBETH's ADVISORS

THEY ARE THE WEIRD SISTERS (meaning the "Prophetic Sisters"). After the opening battle, Macbeth and his friend Banquo encounter the sisters, who impart three important prophecies.

The first two predictions are for Macbeth: he will be promoted to Thane of Cawdor and later to King of Scotland. The third prediction is for Banquo: he will father kings, though he himself will never be king. These trigger in Macbeth's mind an unbridled thirst for the throne, quenched only by the murder of the king.

FAIR
IS FOUL

After the murder of the king, Macbeth consults the sisters in an attempt to learn more of his future. They bring forth three apparitions who provide Macbeth with three more riddling prophecies: beware Macduff; beware no man born of woman; remain invincible until Birnam Forest marches against Dunsinane.

FUSION
The sisters are a confluence of traditions: the sister Fates of Greek mythology responsible for the destinies of humankind; vaporous demonic spirits who appear and disappear at will; and familiar bearded witches who brew trouble in their foul cauldrons.

COME YOU SPIRITS

That tend on mortal thoughts, unsex me here,
And fill me from the crown to the toe top-full
Of direst cruelty! make thick my blood;
Stop up the access and passage to remorse,
That no compunctious visitings of nature
Shake my fell purpose, nor keep peace between
The effect and it!

1.5.41-48

ANSWER
Macbeth is Thane of Glamis. Later, he will become Thane of Cawdor.

QUESTION
What are the Weird Sisters' first two predictions for Macbeth? (ANSWER ON PAGE 21)

THIS IS MACBETH's WIFE

LADY MACBETH AND HER husband share a deep, intimate partnership fueled by their powerful social ambition. In a letter, Macbeth calls her "dearest partner of greatness."

Lady Macbeth believes that her husband is not ruthless enough to murder the king and, in fact, Macbeth does waver in his resolve. On the night of the murder, Lady Macbeth goads him forward by calling his manhood into question and saying she would do it were she a man.

OUT, DAMN SPOT

After the coronation, Lady Macbeth and her husband grow increasingly distant as she begins a steady decline into madness. She is last seen sleepwalking while speaking semi-coherently about the murder and trying obsessively to wash her hands of imagined blood. Haunted by her guilt, she eventually kills herself.

GENDER
Lady Macbeth becomes a human counterpart to the ambiguously-gendered sisters. For example, she calls upon spirits to "unsex" her so she can ruthlessly pursue the regicide; she tells Macbeth she would bash the skull of her nursing child if she gave her word she would do so; finally, she constantly calls her husband's manhood into question.

BLOOD
After the murder, Lady Macbeth says, "a little water clears us of this deed." In reality, however, Lady Macbeth becomes obsessed with washing her hands of their imaginary blood—an apt metaphor for her guilt. A bloody hand will therefore be our shorthand symbol for her.

CHARACTERS | Macbeth's circle | 19

A SUMMARY of MACBETH's CIRCLE

wife

Lady Macbeth
QUEEN BY MURDER

Macbeth's ambitious wife. They share a deep partnership with roots in social advancement rather than love. She masterminds the details of the murder while goading Macbeth forward in his intent to murder Duncan. After the coronation banquet, she and Macbeth grow increasingly distant. She sleepwalks while speaking semi-coherently of the murder and attempting to wash her hands of imaginary blood. Haunted by guilt, she kills herself.

Macbeth
KING BY MURDER

Macbeth's story is dominated by his attempts to force destiny: first, murdering to ensure his predicted coronation, then murdering again to protect his crown. For the latter, Macbeth commits the clumsy post-regicide murders of Banquo and the family of Macduff. He takes solace in the final two apparitions. Unfortunately, Malcolm's army advances behind tree branches and Macbeth is beheaded by Macduff, who was born by Cesarean section.

bloody hand

floating dagger

advisors

Weird Sisters
PROPHETIC HAGS

The ambiguously-gendered sisters predict Macbeth's promotion from Thane of Glamis to Cawdor and his future coronation as king. The first prediction comes true, so Macbeth forces the second with regicide. The sisters also predict Banquo will father kings, so Macbeth has him killed, although his son Fleance escapes. The sisters conjure three apparitions, who riddle Macbeth's future overthrow, as well as a procession of eight future kings from the lineage of Banquo.

 *fiery cauldron*

ANSWER The Weird Sisters first predict Macbeth will be Thane of Cawdor, then King of Scotland.

Royal *family*

The royal family—except Donalbain, who plays a far less significant role than his brother—represents the pragmatic emergence (Duncan's death) and resolution (Malcolm's return) of the dramatic imbalance in the play. That is to say, Duncan and Malcolm represent the extrinsic boundary conditions for the action. Duncan is seen as a surmountable obstacle standing between Macbeth and his unnaturally foretold destiny. However, once the regicide becomes a reality, the natural world shifts on its balance point, in desperate need of restitution. Malcolm is, of course, the man for the job. With political facility, he commands his borrowed army toward Dunsinane, metaphorically moving a forest against the overconfident tyrant. The play ends with Malcolm's unsympathetic eulogy and presumably restorative coronation at Scone.

SONS, KINSMEN, THANES,

*And you whose places are the nearest, know
We will establish our estate upon
Our eldest, Malcolm, whom we name hereafter
The Prince of Cumberland; which honour must
Not unaccompanied invest him only,
But signs of nobleness, like stars, shall shine
On all deservers. From hence to Inverness,
And bind us further to you.*

1.4.36-44

QUESTION
How does Lady Macbeth die? (ANSWER ON PAGE 26)

THIS IS THE KING OF SCOTLAND

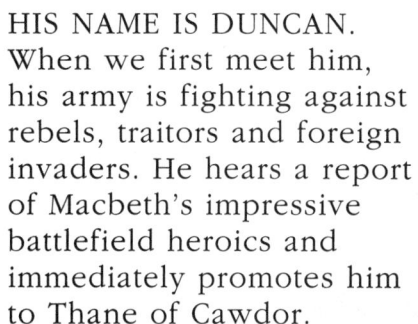

HIS NAME IS DUNCAN. When we first meet him, his army is fighting against rebels, traitors and foreign invaders. He hears a report of Macbeth's impressive battlefield heroics and immediately promotes him to Thane of Cawdor.

King Duncan names his son Malcolm heir to the throne, which only accelerates Macbeth's desire to force the sisters' prophecy to fruition. Duncan invites the thanes to Macbeth's castle at Inverness for a victory celebration the following day.

A MOST
SAINTED KING

Macbeth removes himself from the party and deliberates the regicide. He believes Duncan is a good king and feels his murder would cause a huge outpouring of national grief. Lady Macbeth bolsters his resolve, however, calling his manhood into question. She drugs the two guards, after which Macbeth kills Duncan with their own daggers.

RESONANCE
The natural world feels the shock wave of Duncan's murder: the sky grows dark, an owl kills a falcon and the royal horses tear at each other's flesh. The Macbeths are also impacted. Macbeth hallucinates and goes on a killing spree; Lady Macbeth sleepwalks while talking of the murder and obsessively tries to wash her hands of Duncan's imagined blood.

THIS TUNE GOES MANLY.

*Come, we go to the king. Our power is ready;
Our lack is nothing but our leave. Macbeth
is ripe for shaking, and the powers above
put on their instruments. Receive what cheer you may;
The night is long that never finds the day.*

4.3.241-246

ANSWER
In Malcolm's final speech, he says it is thought that Lady Macbeth took her own life.

QUESTION
Where does King Duncan celebrate his army's victory? (ANSWER ON PAGE 28)

THIS IS PRINCE
MALCOLM

HE IS DUNCAN'S ELDEST SON, the Prince of Cumberland (meaning heir to the Scottish throne, much like the English Prince of Wales). He is named heir the same day Macbeth is honored by King Duncan.

On the night of his father's murder, Malcolm and his brother flee Inverness—Malcolm to England and his brother to Ireland. Malcolm is well received by Edward the Confessor, King of England, who supplies Malcolm with an army.

LET GRIEF
CONVERT TO ANGER

Malcolm leads the army in an attack on Macbeth's position at Dunsinane in eastern Scotland. As they make their way through Birnam Forest to Dunsinane, Malcolm directs the soldiers to cut branches for camouflage, thereby fulfilling the third apparition's prophecy. After Macbeth is beheaded, Malcolm is hailed as King of Scotland.

ASTUTE
When he is asked by a prominent thane to bring an army against Macbeth, Malcolm pretends to be without virtue. He reasons that if the thane is setting a trap for him, then he will ignore Malcolm's statement. If, however, the thane is truly concerned with the fate of Scotland, he will question Malcolm's worthiness to rule. The thane passes Malcolm's impromptu test and is taken into his inner circle.

LION
The courageous lion of Scotland—depicted in red on a background of gold on the Scottish flag—will be our shorthand symbol for Prince Malcolm.

CHARACTERS | Royal Family | 27

TO IRELAND, I;
our separated fortune
Shall keep us both the safer. Where we are,
There's daggers in men's smiles. The near in blood,
The nearer bloody.

2.3.134-137

ANSWER
King Duncan celebrates his victory at Inverness castle, home of Macbeth.

QUESTION
Which English king provides Malcolm with an army? (ANSWER ON PAGE 31)

THIS IS THE OTHER PRINCE

HIS NAME IS DONALBAIN and he is the youngest son of King Duncan. He is seen in the beginning of the play, up until the morning after his father's murder.

After the house is alerted to the news that King Duncan has been murdered, Prince Donalbain and his brother Malcolm enter the courtyard. Donalbain asks what is amiss and Macbeth answers, "You are, and do not know't," hinting the princes are suspects.

WHAT
IS AMISS?

Once the thanes agree to dress and meet in the Great Hall to discuss the king's murder, the princes agree to flee immediately. Donalbain suggests they each go their own way for greater safety. Malcolm decides on England, Donalbain on Ireland.

ABSENCE
Once Donalbain flees to Ireland, he is never seen in the play again. When Thane Caithness deserts Macbeth to join Malcolm's army, he asks Thane Lennox if Donalbain is with his brother. Lennox answers that he is not. Historically, after Malcolm's death, Donalbain attempted to set up a pagan government that opposed his brother's modern reforms.

CHARACTERS | Royal Family

A SUMMARY of the ROYAL FAMILY

king

Duncan
KING OF SCOTLAND

Father of Malcolm and Donalbain. Duncan rewards Macbeth's battlefield heroics by promoting him to Thane of Cawdor. The king holds a victory celebration at Inverness the following evening. Following the party, Macbeth murders Duncan—a good king by Macbeth's own admission—in his bed. Resonances of the regicide are felt in the natural world. Lady Macbeth obsessively tries to wash Duncan's imagined blood from her hands.

crown

eldest son   *younger son*

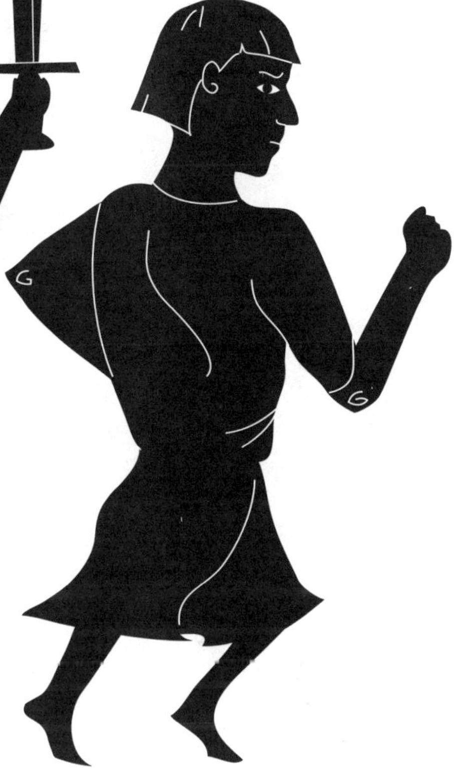

Malcolm
CROWN PRINCE

Malcolm is named Prince of Cumberland (meaning, heir to the throne) on the day Macbeth is honored for his battlefield heroics. After his father's murder, Malcolm flees to England where he is welcomed into the court of Edward the Confessor. King Edward supplies Malcolm with an army of ten thousand men. Malcolm orders the men to cut branches from Birnam Forest for camoflage from Macbeth's scouts. After Macbeth is killed, Malcolm is hailed as king.

lion of Scotland

Donalbain
PRINCE

Of far less consequence to the plot than his brother Malcolm, Prince Donalbain suggests they each go their separate ways after their father's murder. When the politically-astute Malcolm chooses England, Donalbain flees to Ireland and is never seen again in the play. His absence from Malcolm's advancing army is definitively revealed by Lennox, who claims to possess a list of all the gentry in its ranks.

Irish clover

ANSWER Edward the Confessor, King of England, provides Malcolm with an army of ten thousand men.

CHARACTERS | Royal Family | 31

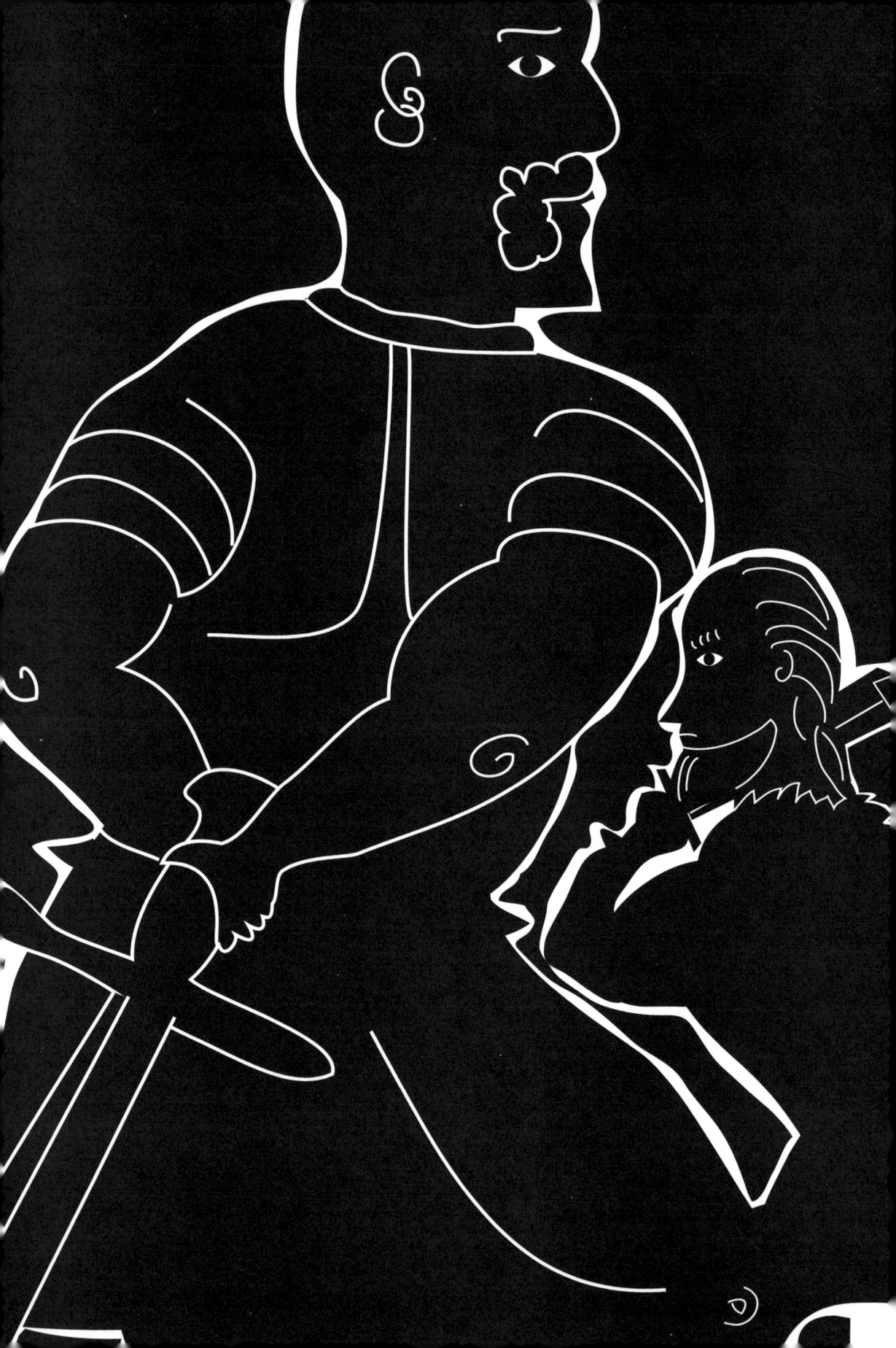

The *Thanes*

The thanes in Macbeth *are depicted as more than simple land barons, they are the barometer for the political health of Scotland. Banquo's murder, almost more than Duncan's, calls into question the integrity of the newly-crowned king. Macduff is first to grow suspicious, snubbing the coronation events and later, after Banquo's murder, pleading with Malcolm to overthrow Macbeth. Ross joins Macduff after the slaughter of Macduff's family. The remaining thanes meet up with Malcolm's army at Birnam Forest. The redemptive event of the play is the transformation of the thanes into Scotland's first earls; the redemptive future of Scotland rests on Fleance's young shoulders.*

MYSELF SHOULD BE
the root and father
Of many kings. If there come truth from them—
As upon thee, Macbeth, their speeches shine—
Why, by the verities on thee made good,
May they not be my oracles as well,
And set me up in hope?

3.1.5-10

QUESTION
Where does Prince Donalbain flee after the murder of his father, King Duncan? (ANSWER ON PAGE 36)

THIS IS MACBETH's COMRADE

HIS NAME IS BANQUO AND HIS son is Fleance. Banquo is a thane who fought bravely with Macbeth against the Scottish rebels and King Sweno of Norway. Banquo was traveling with Macbeth when the sisters uttered their first prophecies.

At that time, Banquo was told he would father kings, yet he would never be king himself. This prediction troubles Banquo as Macbeth is troubled by his, though Banquo has the ethical composure not to act upon it. After his coronation, Macbeth hires three men to murder Banquo and Fleance while they are out riding. Banquo is stabbed twenty times in the head, but Fleance escapes to safety.

SUCCESSION
Macbeth also sees the ghost of Banquo pointing at the procession of kings as conjured by the Weird Sisters. Banquo mocks Macbeth as the eight kings from his lineage pass by to prefigure the fulfillment of the sisters' prophecy. The fertile tree will be our shorthand symbol for Banquo.

THOU SHALT GET KINGS

At the coronation banquet that evening, Macbeth sees a vision of the bloody Banquo seated at the table. As he reacts to it, Lady Macbeth apologizes for her husband's behavior, saying his fit will soon pass.

CONFUSION NOW HATH
made his masterpiece.
Most sacrilegious murder hath broke ope
The Lord's anointed temple, and stole thence
The life o' th' building!

2.3.61-64

ANSWER
Prince Donalbain flees to Ireland after the death of his father, King Duncan.

QUESTION
When does the ghost of Banquo first appear to Macbeth? (ANSWER ON PAGE 38)

THIS IS MACBETH's NEMESIS

HIS NAME IS MACDUFF AND he is the Thane of Fife, an area in eastern Scotland. Macduff's ominous knocking on the south entrance of Inverness unnerves the Macbeths as they rush to wash their bloody hands and change into their nightclothes.

Macduff comes to wake the king for his journey. When he goes to Duncan's room, he is horrified to find the king has been murdered. Later, Macduff chooses not to attend Macbeth's coronation, but instead he decides to travel to Fife and then on to England to join Malcolm.

UNTIMELY RIPPED

In the final scene, Macduff—fighting in Malcolm's army—confronts Macbeth, who tells him he cannot be killed by any man born of woman. Macduff reveals he was born by Cesarean section, thereby shaking Macbeth's confidence. He then kills Macbeth, placing his head on a pole and presenting it to Malcolm.

PATRIOT
Macbeth sends men to kill Macduff's wife, child and servants while he is away in England. When he hears the news, Macduff laments that he cannot hurt Macbeth reciprocally, since Macbeth has no child. In this way, Macduff's personal vendetta is blunted and his killing of Macbeth is depicted more as an act of patriotism than an act of private vengeance.

EXAMINATION
When he first meets Malcolm in England, Macduff's true motives are put to test. Malcolm deceives Macduff into thinking Malcolm has no virtues and should therefore not be king. After Macduff says so, Malcolm believes Macduff's intentions are not evil and he then tells Macduff the truth.

L: **THE NIGHT**
has been unruly. Where we lay,
Our chimneys were blown down and, as they say,
Lamentings heard i' th' air, strange screams of death,
And prophesying with accents terrible
Of dire combustion and confused events
New hatched to the woeful time.

2.3.49-54

R: **ALAS, POOR COUNTRY**
Almost afraid to know itself. It cannot
Be called our mother, but our grave, where nothing,
But who knows nothing, is once seen to smile...

4.3.166-169

ANSWER
The ghost of Banquo first appears to Macbeth at his coronation banquet.

QUESTION
Who kills Macbeth? (ANSWER ON PAGE 41)

THESE ARE LOYAL THANES

ROSS AND LENNOX ARE TWO loyal thanes of Scotland. They function throughout the play as a sort of barometer for public opinion. They are more acceptng of Macbeth's kingship than Macduff—or at least slower to act on their skepticism.

For example, Ross discusses the strange weather and animal behavior with Macduff the day following the regicide. After their conversation, Ross chooses to attend the coronation events, while Macduff instead goes to Fife, then to England.

NOW IS
THE TIME OF HELP

After the murder of Banquo, Ross goes to see Macduff in England, first stopping to speak with Macduff's wife. He brings word to Macduff that his family has been slaughtered and he begs Malcolm to lead an army against Macbeth. The younger Lennox joins up with Malcolm's army later, as it approaches Birnam Forest. Both thanes fight against Macbeth in the final battle.

CRESTS
The crest of Ross is the triple lions; the crest of Lennox is the four roses. These ancient family insignias will be our shorthand symbol for the two loyal thanes.

A QUICK REVIEW of

Weird Sisters
- Prophetic hags
- Ambiguously gendered
- Mythological, demonic and folkloric
- Foretell Macbeth's advancements
- Mysterious
- Foretell Banquo's destiny
- Become Macbeth's dark advisors
- Conjure three riddling apparitions, two of which give Macbeth a false sense of security

Macbeth
- Courageous on the battlefield
- Husband of Lady Macbeth
- Promoted from Thane of Glamis to Thane of Cawdor
- Murders King Duncan in bed
- Crowned King of Scotland
- Has Banquo murdered, but fails to kill Fleance
- Plagued with insomnia and hallucinations
- Has Macduff's family and servants murdered
- Beheaded by Macduff
- Believes he is invincible according to the words of the apparitions

Lady Macbeth
- Wife of Macbeth
- Becomes queen by murder
- Strong willed and ambitious
- Masterminds the details of the murder
- Becomes obsessed with washing Duncan's imagined blood from her hands
- Sleepwalks while speaking semi-coherently about the murders
- Commits suicide

Banquo and Fleance
- Fights courageously alongside Macbeth
- Foretold he would father kings, but never be king himself
- Thane
- Father of Fleance
- Murdered by Macbeth's henchmen
- His ghost haunts Macbeth's banquet
- His ghost points at the procession of kings to mock Macbeth
- Escapes

the Minor characters

Many of the minor characters in Macbeth are interchangeable, serving primarily as a means to make observations about the action. For example, the thanes Menteith, Angus and Caithness do not distinguish themselves as unique. The servants—except Seyton, who possesses a significance based primarily on a pun of his name—announce without distinction the actions which would be difficult to stage. Lady Macduff, however, provides a vulnerable, feminine contrast to the dominant, masculine Lady Macbeth. Old Siward is cast as a consummate soldier and his son dies the only death that would suit his father—death on the battlefield, with wounds in front of his body. Lastly, the enemies (who are never seen, but much spoken of) highlight the overt dangers Duncan is dealing with as king and the prowess of Macbeth's fighting skills.

NO SOONER JUSTICE HAD,

with valor armed,
Compelled these skipping kerns to trust their heels,
But the Norweyan lord, surveying vantage,
With furbished arms and new supplies of men,
began a fresh assault.

1.2.29-32

QUESTION
Who brings Macduff the news his family and servants have been slaughtered? (ANSWER ON PAGE 46)

THE ENEMIES

MACDONWALD
The rebel
Supported by numerous Irish mercenaries from the Western Isles, Macdonwald, a rebellious Scot, wages war against the armies of King Duncan. The fighting is a grueling stalemate until Macbeth hacks his way through the troops to face the rebel. Macbeth then slashes Macdonwald from his navel to his jaw and sets his head upon the castle walls.
Beheaded by Macbeth

KING SWENO OF NORWAY
The rival
Assisted by the Thane of Cawdor, King Sweno of Norway leads a vast army against King Duncan, attempting to capitalize on the exhaustion of Duncan's army after fighting Macdonwald's rebels. Following what seems a certain victory, he is defeated due to the heroics of Macbeth and Banquo. Sweno requests a peace treaty. He is required to pay the enormous sum of $10,000 at St. Colme's Inch before being allowed to bury his dead.
Defeated by Macbeth

CAWDOR
The traitor
A trusted thane of King Duncan, Cawdor assists King Sweno in his battle against Scotland (the type of assistance is unspecified). Upon hearing of Cawdor's treasonous acts, Duncan orders his execution. We later hear an account of the execution, in which Cawdor confesses his treason and begs forgiveness. Macbeth is awarded his title of Thane of Cawdor.
Executed by Duncan

WHITHER SHOULD I FLY?

I have done no harm. But I remember now
I am in this earthly world, where to do harm
Is often laudable, to do good sometime
Accounted dangerous folly. Why then, alas,
Do I put up that womanly defense,
To say I have done no harm?

4.2.69-75

ANSWER
Ross reluctantly tells Macduff his family and servants have been slaughtered.

QUESTION
Who is beheaded by Macbeth in Act One? (ANSWER ON PAGE 48)

THE MURDERERS

THREE MURDERERS
Banquo's killers
Fearing the prophecy that Banquo will father kings, Macbeth hires murderers to kill him and his son, Fleance. Inciting the murderers to the task, Macbeth convinces them Banquo is the cause of all their problems. They successfully murder Banquo, but Fleance escapes. Later, one of the murderers appears at Macbeth's coronation banquet with blood on his face. Macbeth discreetly commends him for a job well done, but is disappointed at Fleance's escape.

MORE MURDERERS
Killers of Macduff's family and servants
Furious at Macduff's flight to England, Macbeth vows to lay siege to the township of Fife, raid Macduff's castle and kill his entire family. Although warned by a messenger, Lady Macduff remains at Fife, alone and unprotected. Soon murderers appear at the castle, killing both Lady Macduff and her young son before dispatching the entire household.

THE MACDUFFS

LADY MACDUFF AND SON OF MACDUFF
The abandoned family
Lady Macduff—a vulnerable, feminine contrast to Lady Macbeth—complains to Ross that her husband has abandoned her and her family. She expresses her fears for their safety as Ross continually defends Macduff's departure. After he leaves, she has a conversation with her young son who remains loyal to his father despite her complaints. A messenger arrives and warns her to flee, but murderers come quickly and slaughter all in the household.

NOW DOES HE FEEL

His secret murders sticking on his hands.
Now minutely revolts upbraid his faith-breach.
Those he commands move only in command,
Nothing in love. Now does he feel his title
Hang loose about him, like a giant's robe
Upon a dwarfish thief.

5.2.17-22

ANSWER
Macdonwald, the rebel Scotsman, is first sliced open and then beheaded by Macbeth on the battlefield.

QUESTION
After Banquo's murder, where does Macbeth speak with his killer? (ANSWER ON PAGE 50)

THE MINOR NOBLES

THANE ANGUS
Loyal to Prince Malcolm
In the first act of the play, Angus, a thane, accompanies Ross as the latter reports to King Duncan of Macbeth's heroics on the battlefield. He and Ross are then sent to tell Macbeth of his promotion to Thane of Cawdor. Ross appears again near the end of the play when, just before the battle at Dunsinane, he eloquently describes Macbeth's desperate situation to his fellow soldiers.

THANES MENTEITH AND CAITHNESS
Warriors for Malcolm
Menteith and Caithness, both Scottish noblemen, are introduced late in the play when they are seen deserting Macbeth to join Malcolm and the English forces. Menteith expresses his confidence in their ultimate victory. Caithness displays zeal for his country by pledging his blood in the fight against Macbeth.

THE LORDS
Revelers at Macbeth's coronation banquet
These guests are among the witnesses to Macbeth's guilty tirade against the ghost of Banquo at Macbeth's coronation banquet. They watch uncomfortably as Macbeth alternates between delusion and reassurance. Eventually, they depart in confusion. Later in the play, Lennox carries on a conversation with an unnamed lord who acts as sounding board for Lennox's sarcastic observations about the events surrounding Duncan's murder.

KNOCK, KNOCK!

*Who's there in the other devil's
name? Faith, here's an equivocator that could
swear in both the scales against either scale,
who committed treason enough for God's sake,
yet could not equivocate to heaven.
O, come in, equivocator.*

2.3.7-11

ANSWER
Macbeth speaks with Banquo's murderer at the coronation banquet,
setting the stage for the entrance of Banquo's ghost.

QUESTION
Who tells Macbeth he has been promoted to Thane of Cawdor? (ANSWER ON PAGE 52)

THE COMMONERS

THE SERVANTS
Announcers of everyone's whereabouts
Servants populating the play are not used as individuals as much as devices for introducing the addition of characters to a scene. When Macbeth's castle is approached by English forces in 5.3, the servant who announces this to Macbeth receives a fierce scolding from the tyrant for being frightened.

THE PORTER
Playing hell's gatekeeper
The Porter provides the only humor found in the play. He appears early the morning following the regicide, responding slowly to a persistent knock which began when Macbeth was cleaning his hands of Duncan's blood. After a night of drinking, the Porter imagines himself to be the keeper of the gates of Hell and describes possible new residents of the netherworld before admitting Macduff and Lennox.

SEYTON
Macbeth's armor-bearer
With his castle about to be attacked, Macbeth calls for his armor. The well-informed Seyton enters and in response to Macbeth's inquiry, he confirms the reports and tells him that the armor is not yet needed. Macbeth, bracing for battle, says he'll put it on anyway and tells Seyton to send out scouts to hang anyone spreading fear. Later, Seyton brings Macbeth the news that Lady Macbeth has died.

OLD MAN
Observer of strange happenings
In keeping with the tradition that nature was affected by the death of kings, the Old Man converses with Ross about the unnatural occurrences that took place during the days surrounding Duncan's death.

IF YOU WILL TAKE
a homely man's advice,
Be not found here. Hence with your little ones.
To fright you thus methinks I am too savage;
To do worse to you were fell cruelty,
Which is too nigh your person. Heaven preserve you!
I dare abide no longer.

4.2.64-69

ANSWER
Angus and Ross are sent by Duncan to bring Macbeth news he is now Thane of Cawdor.

QUESTION
What does the porter playact as he goes to answer the door? (ANSWER ON PAGE 54)

THE MESSENGERS

OFFICER
News from the battlefront
The badly wounded officer provides a detailed recounting of the action on the battlefield, centering mostly on Macbeth's valor. Malcolm points out that the officer himself is a hero, saying the man protected him from certain capture by the enemy. The officer is commended and taken to a surgeon.

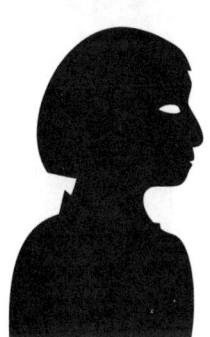

LETTER-BEARER TO LADY MACBETH
News from Macbeth
This unseen, unheard and unspoken-of character brings a letter to Lady Macbeth from her husband who is returning from battle. In the letter, Macbeth describes in detail the prophecies of the Weird Sisters. The ambitious Lady Macbeth joyfully receives the news, however in soliloquy, expresses concern about her husband's ability to seize the kingship.

MESSENGER TO LADY MACBETH
Announces Duncan's visit
Immediately after reading the letter from Macbeth, a messenger appears and informs a servant that the king will be arriving that very evening. Lady Macbeth is at first disbelieving when she hears the news, but she soon learns that the messenger was sent by Macbeth and arrived so out of breath that he could barely deliver his message. Lady Macbeth orders him to be attended to, since he brought such good news.

MESSENGER TO LADY MACDUFF
Announces her danger
A kind stranger warns Lady Macduff of immediate danger to her and her household. In a hurried speech, he pleads with her to take her children and flee. Lady Macduff, frightened and abandoned by her husband, cannot imagine where to go and is murdered shortly after the messenger departs in haste.

CHARACTERS | The Minor Characters | 53

THE TIME APPROACHES
*That will with due decision make us know
What we shall say we have and what we owe.
Thoughts speculative their unsure hopes relate,
But certain issue strokes must arbitrate.
Towards which, advance the war.*

5.4.16-21

ANSWER
As he answers the ominous knocking, the porter playacts he is the doorman at the gates of hell.

QUESTION
How does Lady Macbeth know that King Duncan is coming to Inverness? (ANSWER ON PAGE 56)

THE ENGLISH

KING EDWARD THE CONFESSOR
Healer of the people
A marked contrast to Macbeth's tyranny, King Edward lovingly heals his people of infirmities that doctors have failed to cure. This mysterious gift is described by Malcolm to Macduff, in addition to King Edward's gift of prophecy and other blessings. Although King Edward has no lines in the play, he is apparently greatly admired by Malcolm, who is provided by Edward with an army of ten thousand men.
Provides Malcolm an army of ten thousand

SIWARD
The consummate soldier
Also much admired by Malcolm is the old soldier Siward ("Seyward" in some texts), Malcolm's own uncle. At the time of Macduff's conversation with Malcolm, Siward has already started toward Scotland with "ten thousand warlike men." Siward is nothing if not a pragmatic soldier—when he finds out his son has died in battle, he only asks if the wounds were in front or behind.
Marshalls the assault on Dunsinane

YOUNG SIWARD
An honorable death
Among the English army led by Malcolm is Siward's young son. Despite his age, Young Siward is a valiant soldier like his father and dies bravely at the hand of Macbeth. Upon hearing the sad news of his son's death, Siward inquires as to the location of the battle wounds. He is told they were all on the front of the body, validating his son's honorable soldier's death.
Last to die at the hands of Macbeth

ROUND ABOUT
*the cauldron go,
In the poisoned entrails throw.
Toad, that under cold stone
Days and nights has thirty-one
Sweltered venom sleeping got,
Boil thou first i' th' charmed pot.*

*Double, double toil and trouble,
Fire burn and cauldron bubble.*

4.1.4-11

ANSWER
After reading the letter sent by her husband, Lady Macbeth is told by messenger that King Duncan is coming to Inverness.

QUESTION
Who is the last to die at the hands of Macbeth? (ANSWER ON PAGE 58)

THE OCCULTICS

HECATE
Goddess of darkness (traditionally depicted with dogs)
Hecate appears to the Weird Sisters and expresses her anger at her exclusion from their diabolical plans. She tells them they can make amends when Macbeth visits them the following morning. Hecate plans to conjure evil spirits who will mask themselves as apparitions and pretend to counsel Macbeth regarding his future. The next morning Macbeth comes and the sisters summon the riddling apparitions Hecate has prepared.

THREE OTHER WITCHES (not the Weird Sisters)
Hecate's dark entourage
These witches appear with Hecate just after the sisters finish their potion. They join the sisters in a song about black spirits and dance around the cauldron at Hecate's command.

THE APPARITIONS
Macbeth's window into a dark future

The apparitions are conjured by the Weird Sisters at the demand of Macbeth. The first is an armored head (representing Macbeth's beheading), saying to fear Macduff; the second is a bloody child (Macduff born via C-section), saying to fear no man born of woman; the third is a crowned child holding a tree (Malcolm, the crown prince, bringing Birnam Forest with his army), saying not to fear until Birnam Forest marches against Dunsinane. The second and third apparitions deliberately mislead Macbeth into a false sense of security.

THE PROCESSION OF KINGS
Banquo's revenge
A procession of eight kings from the lineage of Banquo follows the apparitions. The ghost of Banquo points at them, mocking Macbeth. The eighth king holds a mirror, presumed to reflect the image of King James in the original performances of the play. (King James was thought to be from the line of Banquo.)

FOUL WHISPERINGS
are abroad; unnatural deeds
Do breed unnatural troubles. Infected minds
To their deaf pillows will discharge their secrets.

5.1.61-63

ANSWER
Young Siward is the last to die at the hands of Macbeth.

QUESTION
Which two apparitions give Macbeth a false sense of security? (ANSWER ON PAGE 61)

THE CAREGIVERS

THE ENGLISH DOCTOR
Describes King Edward's healing power
Immediately after Malcolm assesses Macduff's loyalty, a doctor enters. Malcolm asks him if King Edward is coming. The doctor says that the king is coming to bestow his healing touch on a group of eagerly awaiting sick. Where medicine fails, the doctor says, the godly Edward uses his gift of healing for his people. This description of the English king immediately follows the discussion of Macbeth's tyranny weighing over Scotland.

THE SCOTTISH DOCTOR
Called by the Gentlewoman
After the murder of Duncan—as Lady Macbeth's guilt steadily overtakes her—she begins sleepwalking. A gentlewoman acting as nurse calls the doctor to corroborate her witness of the queen's night ramblings. The Scottish doctor waits for two nights before seeing for himself the sleepwalking queen. He takes notes as Lady Macbeth mimics hand washing and makes chilling remarks about the murders of King Duncan, Banquo and Lady Macduff. The doctor confesses that Lady Macbeth needs divine more than medical assistance. He later speaks with Macbeth, telling the king that his wife's mental state is beyond his skill as a physician.

THE GENTLEWOMAN
A reluctant witness
Gentlewomen and women of nobility were often employed as ladies-in-waiting to the queen. This Scottish gentlewoman is concerned for her own safety when she hears Lady Macbeth's guilty murmurings during her fits of sleepwalking. The gentlewoman calls upon the services of the Scottish doctor as much for medical advice as for a corroborative witness.

A QUICK REVIEW *of*

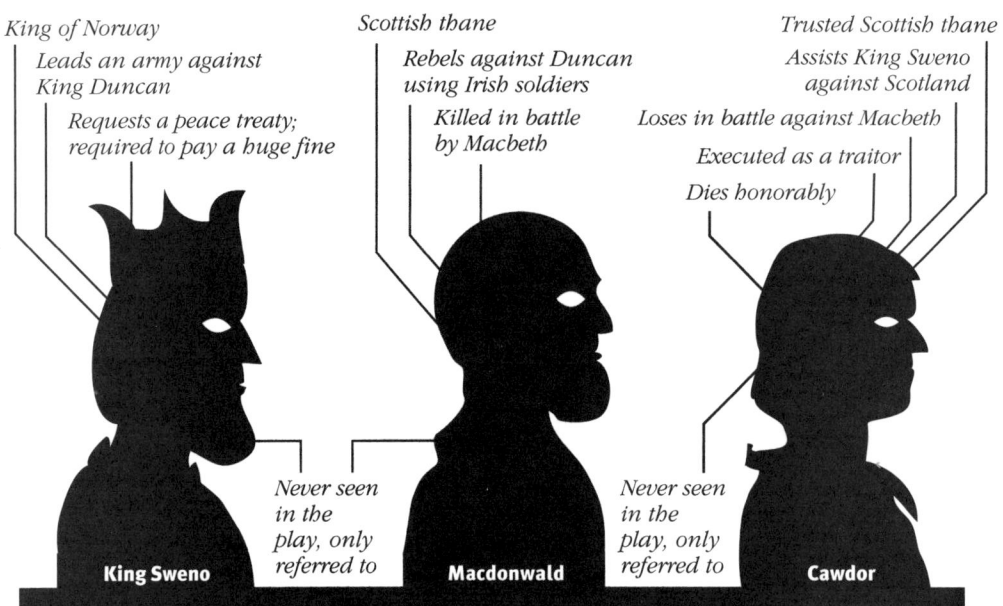

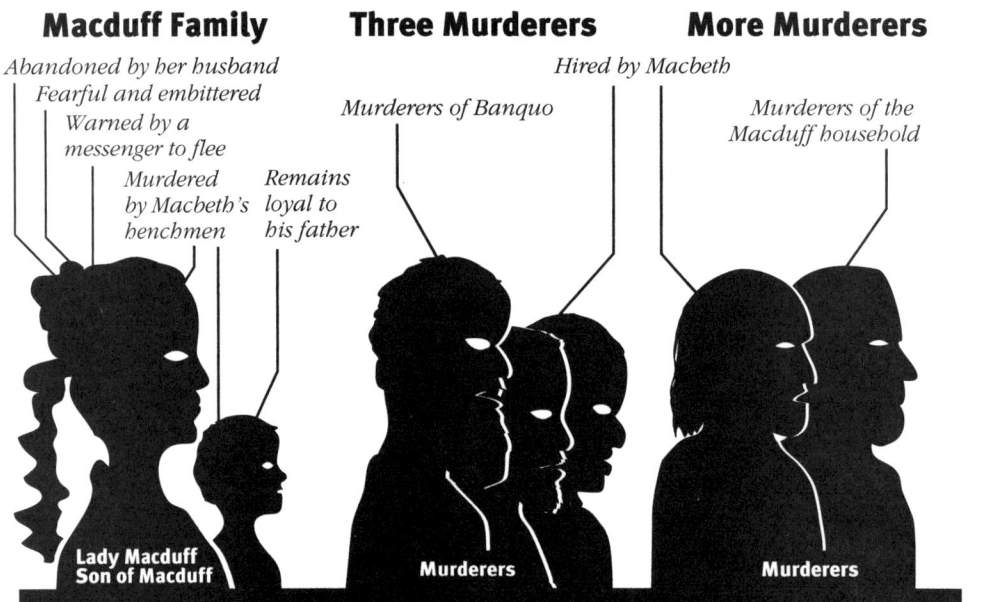

THE MINOR CHARACTERS

The Minor Nobles

Angus
- Loyal to Prince Malcolm
- Accompanies Ross to give Duncan a battle report
- Is among Malcolm's army at end of play

Thanes Menteith and Caithness
- Join Malcolm's army against Macbeth
- Confident in a victory
- Zealous for Scotland

Lords
- Guests at Macbeth's banquet
- Witnesses to Macbeth's outburst against the ghost of Banquo
- They eventually depart the banquet in confusion

The Messengers

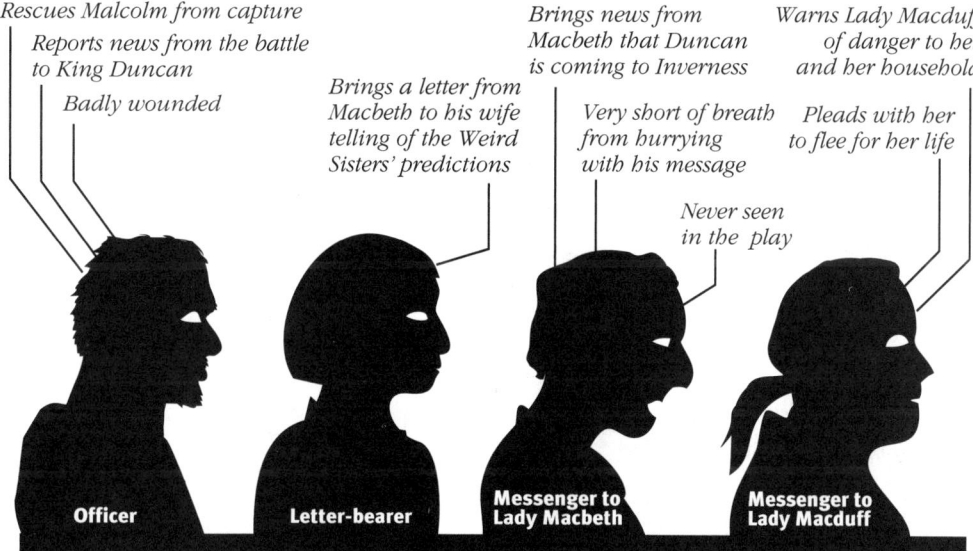

Officer
- Rescues Malcolm from capture
- Reports news from the battle to King Duncan
- Badly wounded

Letter-bearer
- Brings a letter from Macbeth to his wife telling of the Weird Sisters' predictions

Messenger to Lady Macbeth
- Brings news from Macbeth that Duncan is coming to Inverness
- Very short of breath from hurrying with his message
- Never seen in the play

Messenger to Lady Macduff
- Warns Lady Macduff of danger to her and her household
- Pleads with her to flee for her life

ANSWER The second and third apparitions give Macbeth a false sense of invincibility—fearing no man born of woman and no vanquishing until Birnam Forest marches against the castle at Dunsinane.

CHARACTERS | The Minor Characters | 61

A QUICK REVIEW of

The Commoners

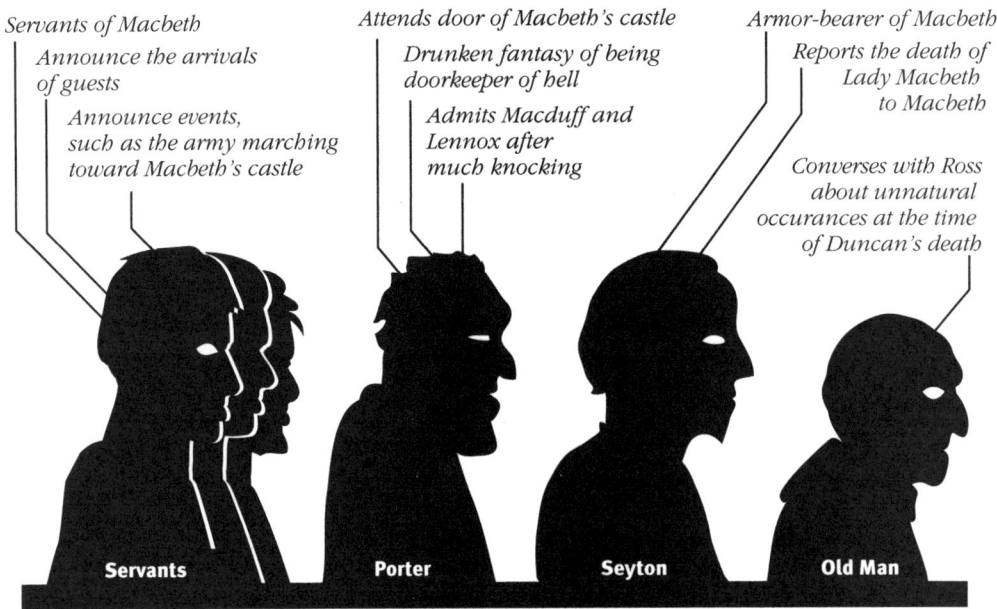

Servants — Servants of Macbeth; Announce the arrivals of guests; Announce events, such as the army marching toward Macbeth's castle

Porter — Attends door of Macbeth's castle; Drunken fantasy of being doorkeeper of hell; Admits Macduff and Lennox after much knocking

Seyton — Armor-bearer of Macbeth; Reports the death of Lady Macbeth to Macbeth

Old Man — Converses with Ross about unnatural occurances at the time of Duncan's death

The English

King Edward the Confessor — Good King of England; Heals his people with touch; Described by Malcolm to Macduff; Never seen in the play, only referred to

Siward — Described by Malcolm as the oldest and best of warriors; Spearheads assault on Dunsinane

Young Siward — Valiant soldier; Dies honorably in battle at the hand of Macbeth

THE MINOR CHARACTERS

The Occultics

Hecate
- Goddess of darkness
- Angered at the Weird Sisters for not including her in their evil plans for Macbeth
- Gives the sisters spirits masked as apparitions to fool Macbeth

Three Witches
- Hecate's entourage
- Join the Weird Sisters in song and dance

Apparitions
- Represents Macbeth's beheading; says to fear Macduff
- Represents Macduff born C-section; says to fear no man born of woman
- Represents crowned prince Malcolm, ordering his army to hide behind branches cut from Birnam Forest; says Macbeth will be invincible until Birnam Forest marches against Dunsinane

Procession of Kings
- Kings from the line of Banquo
- Final king holds a mirror

The Caregivers

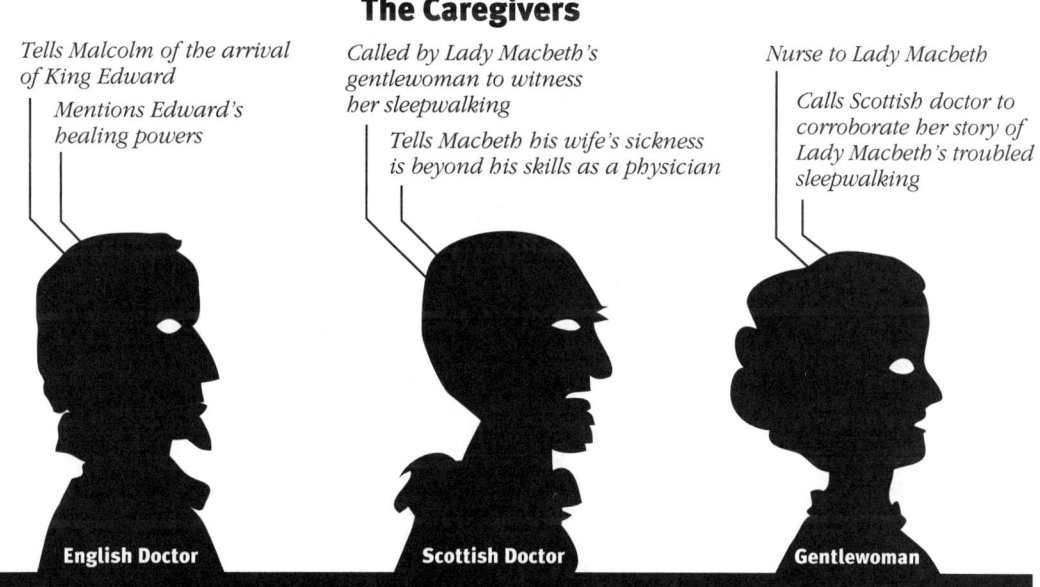

English Doctor
- Tells Malcolm of the arrival of King Edward
- Mentions Edward's healing powers

Scottish Doctor
- Called by Lady Macbeth's gentlewoman to witness her sleepwalking
- Tells Macbeth his wife's sickness is beyond his skills as a physician

Gentlewoman
- Nurse to Lady Macbeth
- Calls Scottish doctor to corroborate her story of Lady Macbeth's troubled sleepwalking

Main
plot

The plot of Macbeth *is divided into two parts by the murder of Duncan. Before the regicide, Macbeth is compelled forward—by his wife and his own ambition—to take his promised destiny by force. Hiding behind the roles of loyal thane and gracious host, he seizes the opportunity to ascend the throne. After the regicide, Macbeth tries in vain to redirect his promised fate, attempting to destroy the generative future (represented by Banquo and Fleance), the political future (represented by Malcolm) and his judicial reckoning (represented by Macduff). He is pragmatically unsuccessful in each case. By his own admission, he ends life unloved, unhonored and unfriended.*

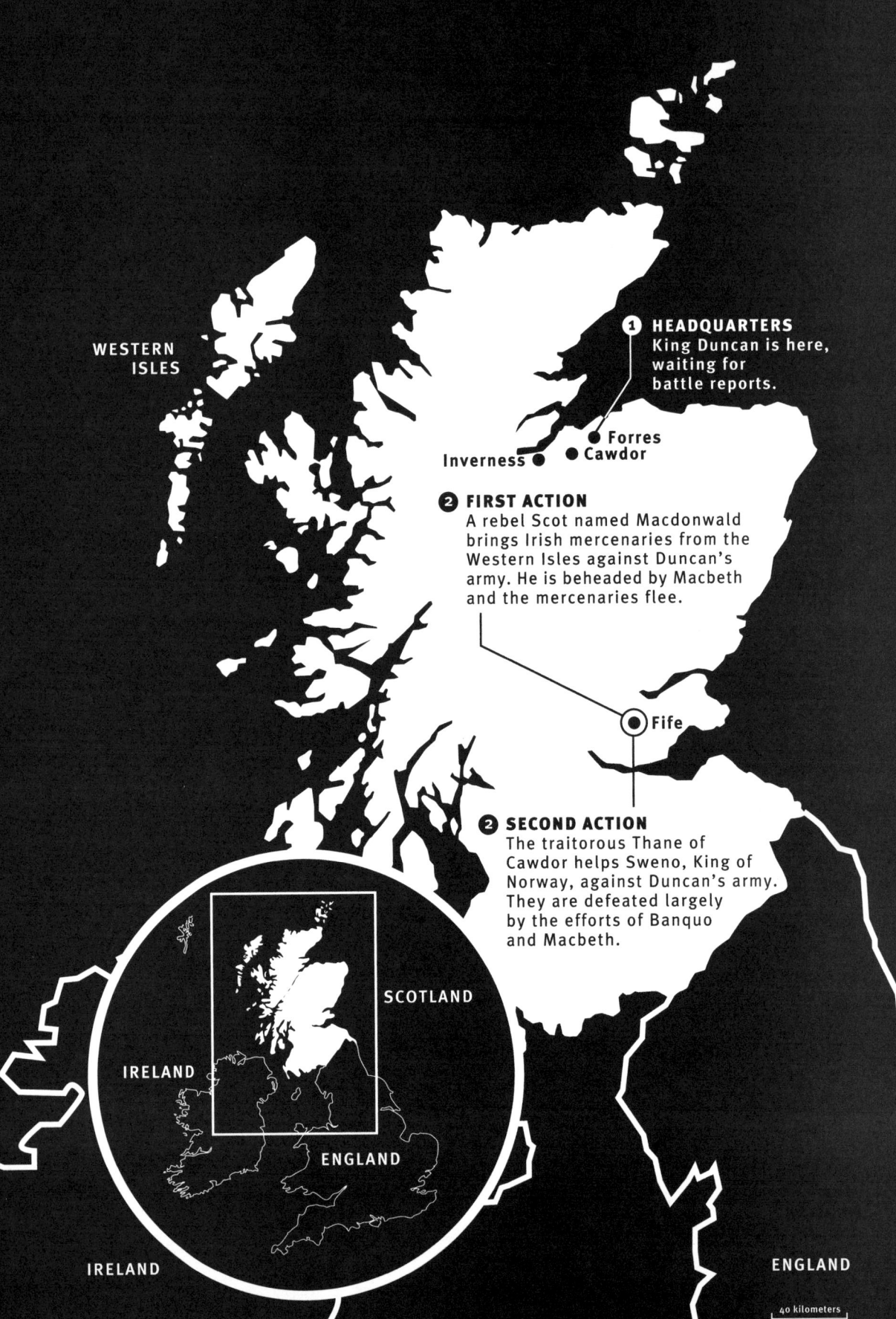

The opening heroics: fighting rebellion, betrayal and invasion.

REBELLION. The first action of Duncan's army is to put down an internal rebellion led by the charismatic Macdonwald. The battle is a stalemate until Macbeth heroically fights his way to confront the rebel leader. Macbeth cuts him open and places his head on the castle walls. The play will be framed by two beheadings: Macdonwald's and Macbeth's.

BETRAYAL. In a betrayal of King Duncan, the Thane of Cawdor assists King Sweno of Norway in his invasion of Scotland (the type of assistance is unspecified). After winning, Duncan has Cawdor executed and gives his title to Macbeth, who will himself betray Duncan. The play thus contains betrayals by two different Thanes of Cawdor.

INVASION. The second action of Duncan's army is to turn back the invading Norwegians, who attacked believing Duncan's army was weakened by its fight against Macdonwald's mercenaries. Again, the battle is won largely through the efforts of Macbeth and Banquo. The play will be framed by two invasions of Scotland: Sweno's and Malcolm's (who is assisted by King Edward of England).

The Weird Sisters plant the seeds of regicide in Macbeth.

FORMATION. The first meeting between Macbeth and the Weird Sisters is on a heath, a wasteland, half-formed like Macbeth's own destiny. The sisters speak of a sailor—a precursor to Macbeth—who will be tormented and sleepless, largely due to the actions of his impudent wife. The dark trio greet Macbeth with successively greater titles—Glamis, Cawdor, King hereafter—showing him his past, present and future, respectively. (The Cawdor title has already been awarded Macbeth, although he has not yet been informed.)

DEATH-IMMORTALITY. Banquo is told he will father kings, but never be king himself. This prophecy, spoken in Macbeth's hearing, seals both Banquo's death and immortality—he is killed by Macbeth's envy, but his progeny reigns over Scotland for generations.

CONFIRMATION. The first of the sisters' prophecies, thaneship of Cawdor, is confirmed with the arrival of Ross and Angus. Like an inverse Oedipus, Macbeth will fantasize about, struggle with and eventually accede to the active fulfillment of his destiny. In short, he will force fate.

1.3–1.4 / The prophecies and their confirmation

Lady Macbeth sets the course for murder.

FORCE OF AMBITION. After reading a letter from her husband telling her of both prophecy and promotion, Lady Macbeth sets an unalterable course for regicide. Connecting herself unknowingly to the ambiguously-gendered, incantatory sisters, Lady Macbeth first invokes spirits to "unsex her" in preparation for the murder. She rightly believes that her husband is "too full of the milk of human kindness" to kill Duncan, another gendered reference.

When Macbeth arrives, Lady Macbeth, worried about her husband's resolve, tells him to leave the murder details in her hands. After Macbeth tells her Duncan plans to leave the next day, she says the sun will never see that morning (it doesn't, literally and figuratively).

When Duncan arrives with his entourage, he ironically remarks on the beauty of Inverness' facade. Lady Macbeth greets him with courtly formality, putting on an effective mask to hide her dark intent. She will remain the dominant intellectual and ambitious force until the coronation banquet. She then goes into decline, demanding bedside candles to throw off the darkness she has called and sleepwalking while trying to wash her hands clean of Duncan's imagined blood.

1.5-1.6 / The prelude to murder

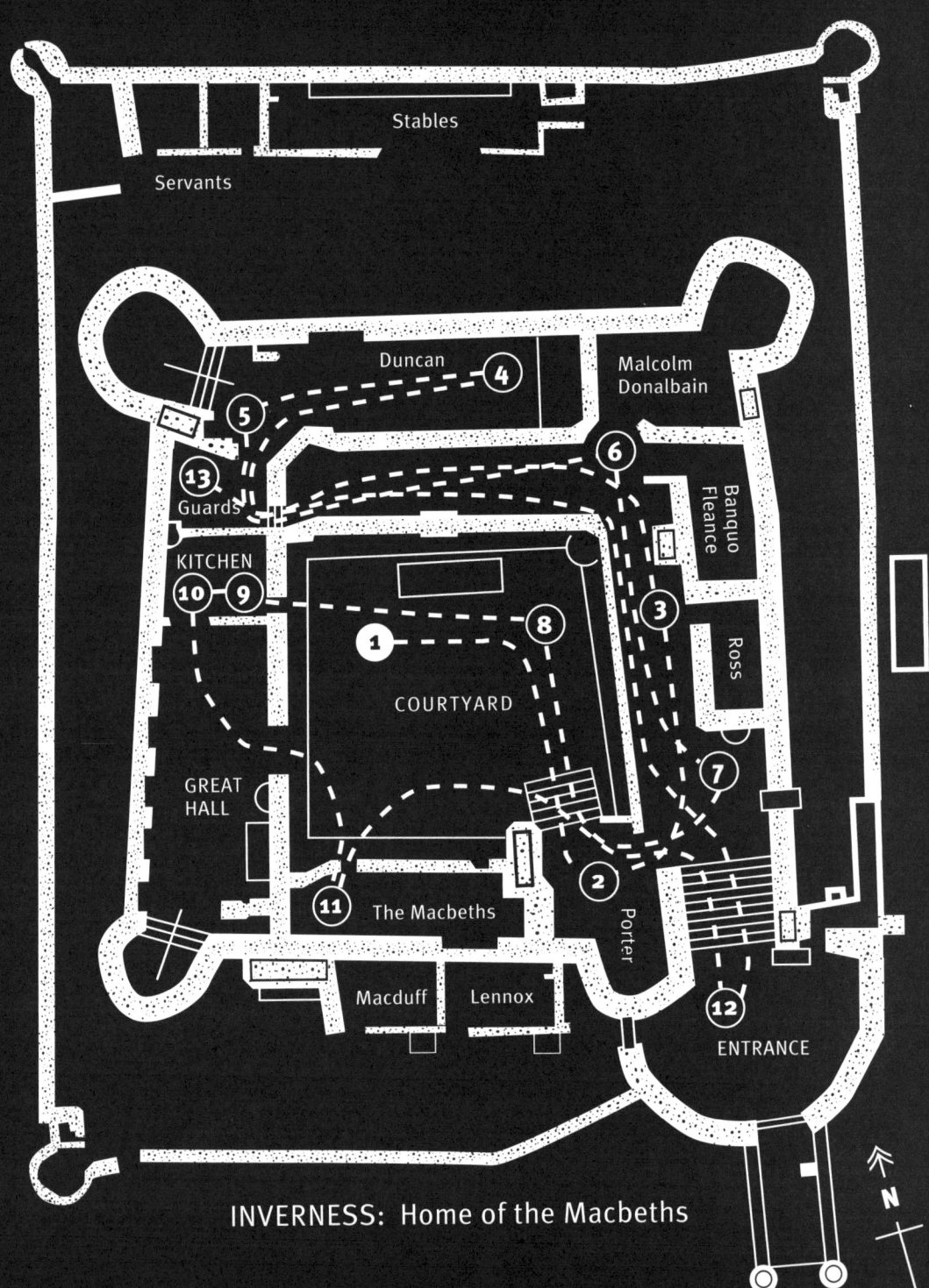

Regicide: how to murder a king.

Now, put yourself in the mind of Macbeth:

1. Supper is nearly over. Lady Macbeth meets you to bolster your failing resolve. You wait until the king retires and Lady Macbeth drugs the guards.
2. Speak with Banquo and Fleance. Send a servant with a coded message to Lady Macbeth: "Ring the bell *when my drink is ready*" (i.e.–*when the guards are drugged*).
3. Hallucinate that you see a floating, bloody dagger. Hear Lady Macbeth ring the bell.
4. Go kill Duncan. Hear an owl shriek as he dies.
5. Smear Duncan's blood on the guards' daggers. Take the daggers with you in your confusion.
6. Hide as Malcolm and Donalbain wake and say their prayers. You want to say, "Amen," but cannot.
7. Imagine you hear voices pronounce: "Sleep no more. Macbeth does murder sleep."
8. Meet and argue with Lady Macbeth. Give her the daggers.
9. Wash your hands as Lady Macbeth returns the daggers and smears blood on the guards.
10. Hear knocking as you scrub the blood from your hands. Lady Macbeth joins you to wash her hands.
11. You and Lady Macbeth change into night clothes.
12. Greet Lennox and Macduff in the courtyard.
13. After Macduff finds the king dead, murder the blood-smeared guards under the pretense of righteous anger.

WESTERN
ISLES

Inverness ● ● Forres
● Cawdor

① ② ③ ④ ⑤

Scone ●

● Fife

⑥

IRELAND   ENGLAND

40 kilometers
25 miles

Counter-movements beyond Macbeth's control arise.

From his coronation until the end of the play, Macbeth switches to a preoccupation with destroying alternative futures, represented chiefly by Banquo, Fleance, Macduff and Malcolm.

1. Donalbain flees to Ireland and is never seen again in the play.
2. Malcolm flees to England where he is welcomed by the court of King Edward the Confessor. Politically astute, Malcolm eventually obtains an army of ten thousand men, raised by Siward, a consummate military leader.
3. Macduff leaves Inverness for Fife, deciding not to attend Macbeth's coronation at Scone or the coronation banquet at Forres.
4. Macbeth is crowned King of Scotland, but Malcolm, having fled, is still alive to challenge his rule.
5. The Macbeths host a coronation banquet at Forres. Before the banquet, Macbeth murders Banquo, but Fleance escapes. Macbeth sees the ghost of Banquo at the banquet and loses composure, causing his thanes to grow suspicious.
6. Macduff goes on to England from Fife, where he joins Malcolm against the tyrannical Macbeth.

4 THE PARADE OF KINGS
Eight rulers from the line of Banquo — the last holding a mirror

Macbeth's disjointed, equivocal glimpses into his future.

PARADE OF APPARITIONS. Like the fabled blind men and the elephant, Macbeth becomes privy to a series of disjointed and apparently contradictory glimpses into his future. After Macbeth demands the sisters reveal their dark mysteries no matter what the consequence, they conjure the spirits Hecate has prepared. The first is an armed head (representing Macbeth's beheading) saying to fear Macduff, the Thane of Fife. The second is a bloody baby (representing Macduff, born by Cesarean section) saying no man born of woman will harm Macbeth. The third is a crowned child holding a tree (representing crowned prince Malcolm carrying Birnam Forest with his army) saying Macbeth will remain invincible until Birnam Forest marches against Dunsinane. Macbeth takes heart in the last two equivocal apparitions, which appear at first glance to nullify the warning of the first.

PROCESSION OF KINGS. The eight kings in the line of Banquo mock Macbeth's infertility and the futility of Macbeth's kingship. (The eighth king held a mirror, presumably to reflect King James' image, who was thought to have been from the line of Banquo.) Macbeth's response to these visions? More murders.

4.1 / Disjointed glimpse into the future

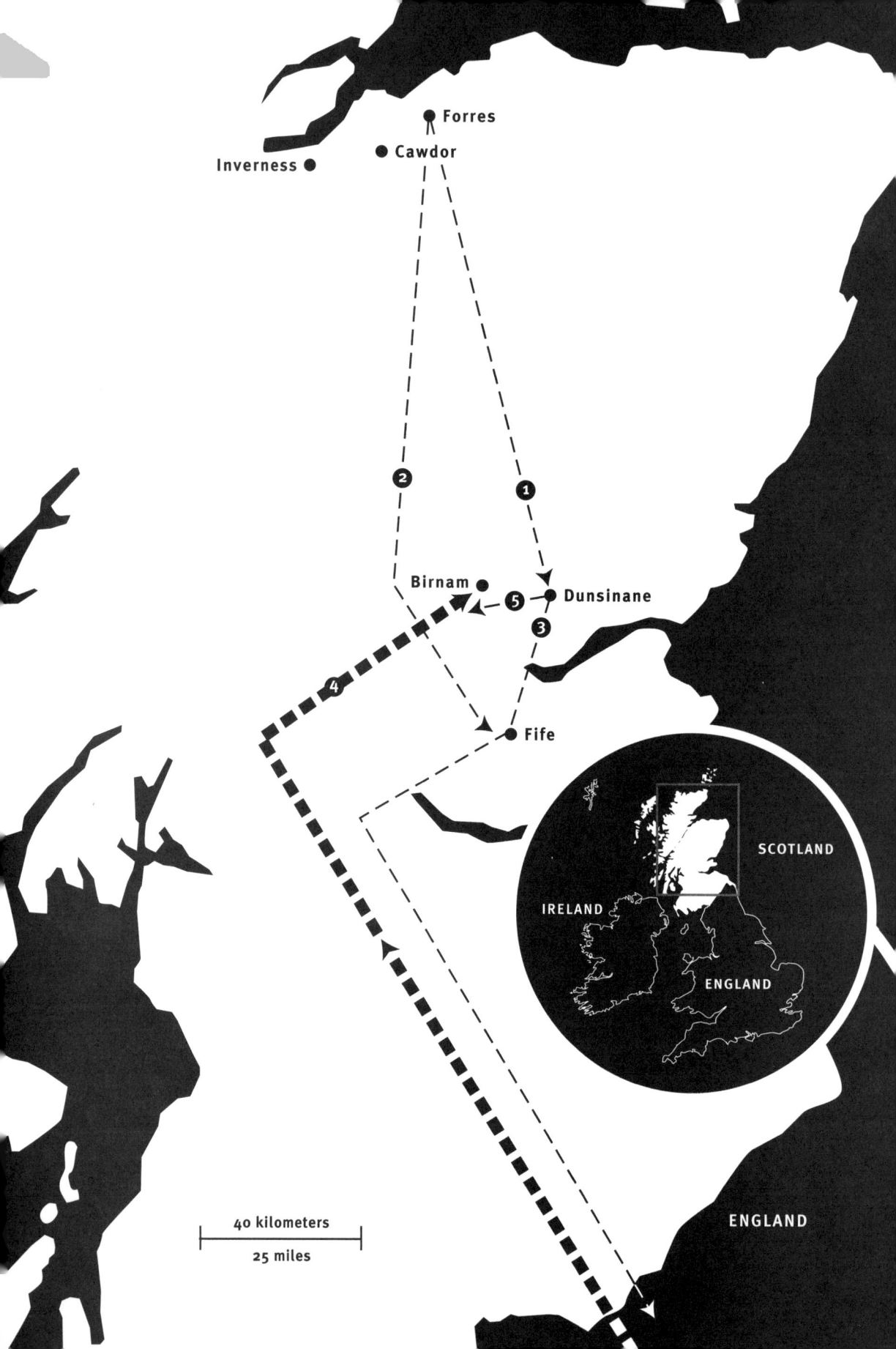

Macbeth's fate finds him at Dunsinane.

The fate Macbeth ruthlessly muscled forward now begins to realign with destiny. After his move to Dunsinane, Macbeth's thanes desert him, his wife commits suicide and he receives news that the forest is marching toward the castle.

1. Macbeth moves from the palace at Forres to the castle at Dunsinane in eastern Scotland.
2. Simultaneously, Macbeth sends murderers to the home of Macduff. The murderers kill Lady Macduff, her children and all their servants. The murders of Macduff's family are even less motivated than the murder of Banquo (who threatened his lineage) and Duncan (who stood in the way of his becoming king).
3. Before the murderers reach the Macduffs, Ross visits Lady Macduff and defends her husband's absence. Ross continues to England, bringing the bad news to Macduff and joining Malcolm's forces.
4. Malcolm's borrowed army of ten thousand marches toward Dunsinane. They carry branches from Birnam Forest for camouflage from Macbeth's scouts. Macbeth hears unbelievable reports of the forest moving.
5. Menteith, Caithness, Angus and Lennox desert Macbeth and join Malcolm's forces at Birnam Forest. Siward leads the assault on Dunsinane, Macbeth is beheaded by Macduff and Malcolm is hailed as king.

Symbols & *themes*

The thematic symbolism within Macbeth *is among the strongest in all of Shakespeare's dramas, perhaps more recognizable owing to the play's brevity. There is a constant framework of theme and symbolic vocabulary—for example, Shakespeare uses the murder of sleep to portray instability and lingering blood to connote the persistence of guilt. Some symbols switch their meaning based on context. Darkness, for instance, first used to symbolize the cloaked suspension of righteousness, remains after the regicide as the first in a series of symbolic imbalances caused by the murder of a king. Also, though far from being a morality play (there is no moral clarification at play's end), Shakespeare did draw upon the Craft Cycle and biblical metaphors, no doubt in deference to his company's new patron, King James.*

Sleep: Macbeth's murder of peace and social stability.

INSOMNIA. Upon murdering Duncan, Macbeth hears a voice cry, "Sleep no more! Macbeth does murder sleep."[1] Macbeth indeed destroys his own peace of mind with the regicide—a fact made evident by his ensuing insomnia.[2] Macbeth believes, after hearing the second apparition's pronouncement, that killing Macduff will doubly soothe his mind and allow him to sleep peaceably once again.[3]

INTERRUPTED. The Macbeth household is awakened by Macduff's call to alarm, signalling the sleeping thanes that their king is dead.[4] Inverness is a microcosm of Scotland, which Ross says will be sleeplessly unstable until Malcolm is once more on the throne.[5]

TROUBLED. Perhaps the most striking example of murdered sleep is Lady Macbeth's incurable, episodic sleepwalking, in which she nightly suffers the self-punishment of continually reliving the details of her crime.[6]

---

[1] 2.2.32-40 [2] 3.2.16-26, 3.4.140-143 [3] 4.1.82-86 [4] 2.3.76-83 [5] 3.6.32-37 [6] 5.1 (all), 5.3.36-54
OTHER REFERENCES 1.3.14-25, 2.1.6-9, 2.1.49-51, 2.2.9-13, 2.2.20, 2.3.35-36.

Babies and children: vulnerability and the loss of innocence.

DEATH. Children are proximal to death in *Macbeth*: Malcolm and Donalbain flee to avoid harm;[1] Fleance narrowly escapes his father's murderers;[2] Macduff's child is killed before his own mother;[3] young Siward is killed in his father's army;[4] the sisters stew the finger of a baby strangled by its parent.[5] Even in metaphor children are unsafe: Lady Macbeth claims she would brain an innocent, nursing child simply because she gave her word on it.[6]

When children are not victims of murder, then they are its harbingers. Macbeth, for instance, imagines an infant cherub trumpeting the murder of Duncan to a sympathetic nation.[7] Two of the apparitions are equivocal representations of Macbeth's own death: the bloody baby[8] and the tree-carrying prince[9]—symbolizing Macduff's unnatural birth and Malcolm's camouflaged army, respectively.

---

[1] 2.3.121-124, 2.3.135-146 [2] 3.3.16-22 (Fleance also represents the generative future.) [3] 4.2.83-85 [4] 5.7.10-13, 5.7 [5] 4.1.30-31 [6] 1.7.54-59 [7] 1.7.21-25 [8] 4.1.86-94 **OTHER REFERENCES** 1.4.23-25, 3.4.102-105, 4.1.151-153, 4.3.5-6, 4.3.176-227, 5.2.9-11, 5.3.4, 5.7.14-16, 5.7.45-46, 5.7.69-73.

Blood and water: heroism and the persistence of guilt.

HEROISM. Blood is first attached to heroism in the service of the state. The wounded officer reports the battle heroics of Macbeth, who fought like he wished to bathe—a function of water—in the blood of the invading Norwegians.[1] The officer's own bloody wounds are commended as honorable by Duncan.[2]

GUILT. The symbolism quickly switches to one of guilt or more specifically, the persistence of guilt. The list of references are overwhelming: the bloody dagger,[3] Macbeth's post-murder lament,[4] Lady Macbeth's smearings on the guards,[5] Banquo's blood on the murderer's face,[6] Banquo's subsequent hallucinatory appearances,[7] and the blood-covered infant apparition,[8] to name only a few. Most prominent, perhaps, is the imagination-produced blood of Duncan on Lady Macbeth's hands. Her subconscious guilt becomes untethered in restless sleep,[9] surfacing as compulsive washing motions that mock her dismissive assessment, "A little water clears us of this deed."[10]

---

[1] 1.2.39 [2] 1.2.43-44 [3] 2.1.45-49 [4] 2.2.18, 2.2.57-60 [5] 2.2.50-55, 2.2.61-62 [6] 3.4.12 [7] 3.4.50-51, 3.4.94, 4.1.122-124 [8] 4.1.76 s.d. [9] 5.1.24-43 [10] 2.2.65 **OTHER REFERENCES** 1.5.43-44, 2.2.44-48, 2.3.102-112, 2.3.140-141, 2.4.4-6, 3.2.48-50, 3.4.74-81, 3.4.121, 3.6.33-35, 4.3.30-41, 5.2.3-5, 5.6.9-10, 5.7.33-38.

Rebellion of nature: the inversion of intrinsic order.

SHOCKWAVES OF REGICIDE. Perhaps the easiest symbolic relationship in the play to recognize is the link between regicide and the subsequent rebellion of nature. After invoking the darkness of hell to shroud their evil deed, Lady Macbeth says, in an unwitting prophecy regarding Duncan's intention to leave Inverness in the morning, "O never / Shall sun that morrow see."[1] Indeed, the following morning (when Duncan's body is removed from Inverness for burial), daylight is hidden in darkness[2]—the royal sun is subverted by the forces of the night. This inversion of the intrinsic natural order—this upset of the divine balance of the universe by the shockwaves of regicide—was a common theme in medieval lore, supported by the biblical assertion that kings received their right to rule directly from God.[3] Ross and the old man also speak of two other inversions: a high-flying falcon is killed by a low-flying owl[4] and the hay-eating royal horses become wild and tear at each other's flesh.[5]

---

[1] 1.5.62-63 [2] 2.4.4-10 [3] See Rom. 13:1-6, I Pet. 2:13-15 [4] 2.4.10-13 [5] 2.4.14-20 OTHER REFERENCES 1.5.44-48, 2.1.49-51, 2.2.6-8, 2.3.49-58, 2.4.27, 3.4.141, 4.2.11, 5.1 (all), 5.5.29-37, 5.7.39-47.

Gender: agression, vulnerability and the human community.

MANHOOD AND AGRESSION. Lady Macbeth invokes the spirits to "unsex" her—that is, to conform her to an agressive paradigm of manhood for the purpose of driving the regicide forward.[1] Her invocation links her to the ambiguously-gendered, bearded sisters and places her in opposition to the vulnerably feminine Lady Macduff (who later haunts her sleepwalks in verse babble: "The Thane of Fife had a wife. Where is she now?").[2] Lady Macbeth also calls her husband's manliness into question: when he tries to withdraw from the idea of regicide,[3] and when he loses composure at the coronation banquet.[4] In the first case, Lady Macbeth tells him that he will only be a man if he goes through with the murder (an argument Macbeth will later use with Banquo's killers[5]). The link between manhood and agression is communal in the play and is not a view held by the Macbeths alone. Malcolm makes this clear when he tells Macduff to convert his grief into anger, using manhood as a repeated justification for re-channeling his emotion.[6]

---

[1] 1.5.40-43 [2] 4.2.73-75, 5.1.36 [3] 1.7.36-58 [4] 3.4.58-60 [5] 3.1.91-108 [6] 4.3.225-241
OTHER REFERENCES 1.3.45-47, 2.3.129-130, 3.4.99, 5.2.9-11, 5.7.47-48, 5.7.69-73.

Clothing: inability to match position or moral equivalence.

INFERIORITY. Clothing is a consistent metaphor of rank. In the play it is used to portray the inability of a person to rise to the demands of a current situation. Macbeth, for instance, after he hears of his promotion, questions Ross and Angus as to why they have dressed him in "borrowed robes," (a borrowed rank) since the Thane of Cawdor is still alive.[1] When in that same scene Macbeth becomes lost in his thoughts, Banquo explains that Macbeth is unused to his new title, which like new clothes must be worn for some time before they become comfortable.[2] Speaking of Scotland, Macduff later hopes that the new robes of Macbeth's kingship don't prove inferior to the old robes of Duncan's reign.[3] Finally, as the thanes are deserting, Angus characterizes Macbeth as a dwarf who has stolen a giant's robe[4]—that is, Macbeth is unable to match either the political greatness or moral goodness of the murdered Duncan.

---

[1] 1.3.110-111 [2] 1.3.144-148 [3] 2.4.38-39 [4] 5.2.20-22 **OTHER REFERENCES** 1.7.31-36, 2.2.61-62, 3.1.107-108, 4.1.86-89, 4.3.24-25, 4.3.29-30, 4.3.45-50, 5.3.50-56 (Macbeth's frantic dressing and undressing in his armor may suggest impatient and reactionary decision-making).

Equivocation: an appropriated tool of treason and murder.

TOPICAL. In 1605, a group of conspirators aiming to kill James I were apprehended before they could ignite 36 barrels of gunpowder beneath the House of Lords.[1] The Jesuit Father Henry Garnet was informed of the plot from a priest under his charge who overheard the lead conspirator's confession. Garnet concealed the privileged information, not wishing to violate the confidentiality of the confessional. After this was discovered, Garnet was arrested and tried for treason. When Garnet was confronted with giving false testimony during the course of his trial, he invoked the Doctrine of Equivocation, which he maintained allowed him to tell misleading or vague half-truths in his defense. Shakespeare thus appropriated the tool of equivocation as a topically-charged symbol, linking the treason against Duncan to the treason against James.

---

[1] Celebrated in England as Guy Fawkes Day. OTHER REFERENCES 1.1.12, 1.3.123-126, 1.5.65-76, 1.6.14-20, 1.7.82, 2.3.8-9 (an inside joke), 2.3.30-32, 4.1 (all; the apparitions are equivocal, giving Macbeth false security.), 4.3.178 (Ross equivocates news of the slaughter.), 5.5.42-45, 5.7.50-53.

Darkness: the cloaked suspension of righteousness.

THE COVER OF NIGHT. Much of the action in the play takes place at night or during daylight which has been strangled out by darkness. Both Macbeth and Lady Macbeth invoke darkness to hide their crime.[1] Banquo reveals the success of their petition the night of the regicide, as he points out the starless night to Fleance.[2] Unfortunately for the Macbeths, the darkness they invoked persists uncomfortably the next morning, beginning the string of unnatural events that follow the regicide.[3] Banquo's murder, like Duncan's, is done in total darkness, as the amateur murderers clumsily extinguish his torch—a mistake that allows Fleance to escape.[4] By the final Act, the incessant darkness haunts a guilt-ridden Lady Macbeth, who orders candles be kept near her at all times.[5] At the news of his wife's death, Macbeth's strangely moving, emotionally bereft eulogy speaks of life in terms of the meaningless interplay between light and shadow.[6]

---

[1] 1.4.52-55, 1.5.51-55 [2] 2.1.4-5 [3] 2.4.4-10 [4] 3.3.20-22 [5] 5.1.18-20 [6] 5.5.22-24 **OTHER REFERENCES** 3.1.135-138, 3.4.126-127, 5.1.30-31.

Biblical Christianity: understanding the audience.

KING JAMES I. To say *Macbeth* is a model for the Christian story is wholly incorrect, nevertheless, the play—the first of Shakespeare's performed for his new, religiously-minded patron, King James I[1]—is replete with Christian symbolism. In Christian terms, Macbeth can be viewed as a reluctant Adam to Lady Macbeth's sin-enticing Eve, whose actions produce the fallen, post-regicide world of darkness and natural rebellion.[2] Duncan, a type of Christ, is seen by Lady Macbeth as her sleeping father.[3] He sleeps in the company of two men, who die just after him, like the biblical two thieves.[4] When the Christ typology is applied to the knocking Macduff—who is anything but Christ after this scene—he arrives at the doorway to Hades (Inverness) accompanied by only one man (Angus), representing the thief of promise;[5] the porter overtly playacts the doorman to Hell. Macbeth ironically dons the full armor of Seyton.[6] Macduff claims his family died for his sins, not for their own and he becomes the triumphant man not born of woman— both inversions of the biblical Christ who was born without the agency of man[7] and died for the sins of all.[8]

---

[1] The same King James to authorize the translation of the bible commonly termed, the King James version. [2] See Gen. 3:17, Jn. 23:44-45, Rom. 8:22 [3] 2.2.12-13, Jn. 14:7 [4] Mt. 27:38, Jn. 19:32 [5] Jn. 23:39-43 [6] Eph. 6:13 [7] 5.7.44-47, Mat. 1:18-20 [8] 4.3.230-233, I Cor. 15:3.

Birds: heralds of death and inverted hierarchy.

DEATH. All of the birds in *Macbeth* are negative symbols, except for the apparently happy house martins that Banquo tells Duncan nest at Inverness.[1] They are themselves emblems of irony. Besides these, birds in the play are cast almost exclusively as heralds of death: most memorably the hoarse raven of Lady Macbeth's murderous resolve[2] and the shrieking owl who announces the moment of Duncan's murder.[3]

HIERARCHY. In a few instances, birds are symbols of hierarchy. For example, a high-flying falcon is seen killed by a low-flying mouse owl in the post-regicidal upheaval of nature,[4] emblematic of King Duncan's murder at the hands of an inferior. Also, Lady Macduff and her son discuss the vulnerability of their situation in terms of "little bird" symbols,[5] which characterize their lowly position. In like manner, Macduff, after hearing of their slaughter, calls Macbeth a hell-kite who has killed all his chickens in one deadly swoop.[6]

---

[1] 1.6.3-10 [2] 1.5.39-41 [3] 2.2.3, 2.3.54-55 [4] 2.4.10-13 [5] 4.2.6-14, 4.2.30-37, 4.2.69 [6] 4.3.221-224
OTHER REFERENCES 1.2.34-35, 3.2.51-54, 3.4.71-73, 3.4.124-126.

Hallucination and illusion: Macbeth's chief preoccupation.

CLIMACTIC MOVEMENT. Though some illusions are recognized by other characters—such as the post-regicide darkness—illusions are, without exception, a continuous preoccupation of Macbeth, whose mind is supremely fit for their production. The force of Macbeth's ambition, for instance, fabricates the floating dagger that guides him to Duncan as easily as the weight of his guilt produces the ghost of Banquo, who usurps his seat at the coronation banquet. Nor are his hallucinations confined to the visual: upon murdering Duncan, Macbeth hears a voice proclaim that he has murdered sleep.[1] The climax of Macbeth's creative imagination is the parade of apparitions, which seem to assume more of a complex dream symbolism than a realistic form. After this illusory apex, the natural world begins to recover and the unnatural, by necessity, takes more explainable constructions: Lady Macbeth is simply delusional; the forest moves as a result of military strategy; Macduff is victorious because he was born via Caesarian section, a common surgical procedure.

---

[1] 2.2.33-38 OTHER REFERENCES 1.1.13, 1.3.53.55, 1.3.80-86, 1.3.139-145, 2.1.57-64, 3.5.26-29, 5.7.19-20.

Fate and free will: consequences of action and ambition.

DESTINY. *Macbeth* is, fundamentally, a struggle between free will and fate, or (in religious terms) a struggle between free will and predestination. After hearing the assurances of his Cawdor promotion, Macbeth embarks upon a quest to accelerate his royal destiny—a sort of inverse Oedipus[1]—bringing about the murder of Duncan and his own ascencion to the throne. After the regicide, however, Macbeth attempts to augment the course of destiny: he orders the murders of Banquo (successfully) and Fleance (unsuccessfully)[2] to nullify their predicted fate of royal progeneration; he wishes to kill Macduff to doubly ensure his own safety.[3] By play's end, Macbeth, his wife, Scotland and the natural world suffer by his exercise of free will to accelerate and then redirect the wheel of destiny. The full consequences of his action and ambition include the murder of his liege and several fellow Scots, the madness and suicide of his wife, the tyranny of his reign and his own beheading.

---

[1] See Macbeth's allusions to eye-plucking (Oedipus' self-punishment) at 2.2.56 and 4.1.113-116. [2] Fleance represents the generative future and so cannot be destroyed. [3] 4.1.82-86 **OTHER REFERENCES** 1.2.16-19, 1.5.25-30, 1.5.69-53, 2.3.150-151, 3.1.74-75, 3.1.120-123, 3.1.148-151, 3.5.16-30, 3.6.27-32, 5.7.18-27.

A QUICK REVIEW *of*

Sleep  Sleep represents peace and social stability. It's destruction is most readily seen in the post-regicide voice Macbeth hears, Macduff's waking of the household at Inverness, Macbeth's ensuing insomnia and the troubled sleepwalking of Lady Macbeth. It is foreshadowed by the sleep-tortured sailor in 1.3.

Babies and children  That children are proximal to death is most apparent in Lady Macbeth's nursing boast, Fleance's witness of his father's murder and the brutal murder of Macduff's son. Also of note are Macbeth's personification of Pity and the final two apparitions—one an infant, the other a child—who equivocally foretell Macbeth's death.

Blood and water  When in the service of the state, blood is a symbol of heroism, such as the officer's wounds in 1.2. The symbol switches to the persistence of guilt upon the murder of Duncan, most visible in Lady Macbeth's compulsive washing motions. Water is ineffective absolution.

Rebellion of nature  Nature is the intrinsic order of the universe and, therefore, the rebellion of nature is the reversal of that order. Examples of this are the post-regicide darkness, the falcon killed by the owl and the wild, flesh-tearing horses. The fulfillment of the apparitions' final two unnatural conditions by natural means sets things right.

Gender  Gender is a symbol most commonly used to demonstrate aggression and vulnerability. Lady Macbeth famously calls for her own gender transformation and continually calls her husband's manhood into question. Lady Macduff, an example of feminine vulnerability, haunts Lady Macbeth's sleepwalks.

Clothing  Clothing is a consistent symbol of rank. It is used most commonly as a means to demonstrate that a character (usually Macbeth) is unable to match the position or moral equivalence of another. As the thanes are deserting *en masse*, Angus characterizes Macbeth as a thieving dwarf in a giant's robe.

the THEMES & SYMBOLS

Equivocation  Equivocation—or misleading half-truth—is a universal theme in Macbeth. It is seen in the smiling appearances the Macbeths assume while plotting the murder of Duncan. The final two apparitions are equivocal, giving Macbeth a false sense of invulnerability. There is also a tie between equivocation and the Gunpowder Plot.

Darkness  Darkness is first invoked by the Macbeths as a cover for their wicked deeds. After the regicide, however, darkness uncomfortably remains, becoming the first in a series of natural imbalances caused by the shockwave of regicide. Lady Macbeth demands constant light beside her as she falls sharply into madness.

Christianity  *Macbeth* is infused with Christian metaphor. Macbeth plays Adam to Lady Macbeth's Eve, producing the unnatural catastrophes of the fallen, post-regicide world. The porter scene is a reenactment of Christ's harrowing of hell. Macduff's innocents are slaughtered. Macbeth dons the full armor of Seyton.

Birds  Most birds in Macbeth are heralds of death, such as Lady Macbeth's hoarse raven and the owl that shrieks to announce Duncan's murder. The house martins of Inverness are symbols of irony. The old man's owl-killed falcon symbolizes inverted hierarchy. The Macduff family is spoken of in vulnerable little birds.

Illusion and hallucination  Macbeth's mind is supremely fit for the production of illusion, such as the floating dagger of ambition and the guilt-produced ghost of Banquo. The high point of illusion is the parade of apparitions and procession of kings. Afterward, the illusions (such as Birnam Forest walking) acquires rational explanation.

Fate and free will  The play is fundamentally a struggle between one man's free will interfering with the mechanics of destiny—and vice-versa. After hearing his predicted future, Macbeth embarks on a dark quest to accelerate his fate; after the regicide, he attempts to destroy all predicted futures and redirect his ultimate destiny.

Scene
by scene

This chapter serves as a summary of the action and dialogue in each scene of the play. The scene breaks in Shakespeare's plays are arbitrary—they were not noted in the original documents—but, except in rare instances, they occur when the stage completely clears. Macbeth *contains many short scenes (especially in Act Five). These, therefore, have been combined onto single summary pages, as with 5.2, 5.3 and others. We reccommend you read this chapter in one or two sittings, if time allows, thereby gaining a large, sweeping view of* Macbeth, *before tackling the actual text of the play.*

ACT 1, SCENE 1

The Weird Sisters plot to meet Macbeth on the barren plain.

IT IS NIGHTTIME in medieval Scotland. The play opens on three cabalistic hags and the clamor of thunder and lightning. They are referred to later by the other characters in the play as the Weird Sisters, meaning the Prophetic Sisters (an allusion to the prophetic Fates of Greek mythology). This is the briefest opening scene of all Shakespeare's plays—only twelve lines—and it establishes the brevity for the entire play, the shortest of Shakespeare's tragedies.

We come upon the sisters as they discuss when they will next meet. The first asks if they should meet in thunder, lightning or rain, abandoning the clocks of society—toll bells or position of the sun—and associating their meeting with powerful natural displays. The second answers that they will meet when the battle raging between the king's army and the rebels is over. Without witnessing the fighting, she describes the battle details (which we learn are correct in the next scene): the battle will appear as if the king has lost, before he emerges victorious.

The third sister prophesies that the fighting will be over before sunset, whereupon the first sister asks where they should meet. The second answers that they will meet on the open moor, an undefined wasteland. The third says—in a tone more of confirmation rather than revelation—they will meet with Macbeth there.

A secondary meaning of "Weird" is "supernatural" and the action that follows supports this definition. Each sister responds to the call of her familiar, or attendant spirit, painting the picture of the sisters as witches. For example, the first sister responds to the call of a cat—a call which only she can hear—with, "I come, Graymalkin." The name Graymalkin was a common name for a cat, especially a witch's familiar. The second sister responds to the call of a toad, also a common familiar. The third sister responds to an unidentified spirit. In their obedient responses, the sisters appear to be servants of these attendant spirits, an inversion of common folklore.

Inversions such as this are thematic in *Macbeth* as in the ensuing chiasmus, "Fair is foul and foul is fair," which establishes an underlying motif for the play: "Good and evil will exchange positions." Macbeth's perceptive comment about the weather and the battle in 1.3.38 echoes this phrase. As though they are one person, the witches drift weightlessly through the murky fog.

FATES
The Weird Sisters in *Macbeth* have strong resonance with the three mythological sisters known as the Fates. For every individual, the thread of destiny was spun by Clotho, measured by Lachesis and cut by Atropos. The decisions of the sisters were immutable.

ACT 1, SCENE 2

King Duncan hears the battlefield reports of Macbeth's heroics.

WHILE THE WEiRD SISTERS prophesy about the outcome of the fighting, King Duncan awaits battle reports in his northern headquarters at Forres. He is with his two sons—Princes Malcolm and Donalbain—as well as Thane Lennox ("thane" is a title equivalent to a baron). An officer enters, bleeding badly and Prince Malcolm recognizes him as one who protected him on the battlefield, fighting bravely to thwart the prince's capture.

The officer provides battle details in the form of two key metaphors. The first metaphor describes the initial stalemate: the army of King Duncan and the mercenary army of his foe—the rebel leader Macdonwald—were like two swimmers who, by clutching each other in the water, cause themselves both to drown. The second analogy describes the victory: Fortune is personified as the smiling mistress of Macdonwald, who in the end proved no match for Macbeth, beloved favorite of personified Valor. Macbeth brutally chopped his way through the fighting until he faced Macdonwald. Macbeth then slit him from his navel to his jaw, cut off his head and placed it on their defensive wall.

King Duncan is delighted at this news and he praises Macbeth as valiant and noteworthy. The officer continues his report concerning a second action that came upon the heels of their victory over the rebel army of Macdonwald. King Sweno of Norway, believing King Duncan's army to be weak from battle, sent a fresh army of his own to overtake them.

Duncan asks if Macbeth and Banquo were shaken by this new assault. The officer answers that, on the contrary, the two were vitalized by the attack and redoubled their efforts, fighting as if they intended to bathe in blood. After giving his report, the officer is too weak to continue. King Duncan commends the officer's bravery and directs servants to take him to a surgeon.

Ross, another of Duncan's thanes, enters with further news from the battlefront. He reports that the Norwegian army was assisted (in an unspecified capacity) by the Thane of Cawdor. He goes on to say that Macbeth led Duncan's army to victory, calling Macbeth the bridegroom of Bellona, the Roman goddess of war.

Ross notes that King Sweno has been forced to pay retribution of ten thousand dollars (an enormous sum) in return for the privilege of burying his dead. Duncan orders the traitorous Thane of Cawdor to be executed and—in fulfillment of the Weird Sisters' prophecy in 1.3—he transfers the thaneship to Macbeth. Ross agrees to greet Macbeth with the new title and leaves to intercept Macbeth on his journey home from the battlefield.

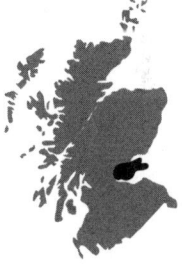

FIFE
King Duncan's army fought two battles in the region known as Fife, shown in black above. Macbeth first gains honor on the battlefields of Fife. Finally, after his regicide and multiple cover-up murders, Macbeth is killed by Macduff, Thane of Fife.

ACT 1, SCENE 3

The prophecies of the Weird Sisters; Macbeth is named Thane of Cawdor.

ON THE HEATH between Fife and Inverness, the Weird Sisters meet. The first sister relates where she has been: a sailor's wife sat eating chestnuts and when the first sister asked her for some, she said, "Leave me alone, witch." The first sister then vows she will curse the woman's husband—she will transform herself into a tailless rat, sail in a sieve to his ship, curse him for 81 days with thirst and insomnia, and pound his ship with ocean storms.

Seeing Macbeth and Banquo approaching, the Weird Sisters hold hands and chant, encircling their cauldron nine times, alternating directions in sets of three. Macbeth says to Banquo he has never seen a day "so foul and fair," commenting on both the extreme change in weather and the sweeping change of fortunes on the battlefield. Banquo catches sight of the Weird Sisters and describes them in equivocal terms as hovering between physical and spiritual, masculine and feminine. Macbeth bids them to identify themselves, but the sisters hail him with his past, present and future titles—Thane of Glamis, Thane of Cawdor, King.

Banquo questions why Macbeth is so startled by the two auspicious predictions (Macbeth does not yet know the title of Thane of Cawdor has been transferred to him). Banquo asks the sisters if they have any predictions for him. They reply that Banquo will be both lesser and greater, unhappier and happier than Macbeth. They prophesy that Banquo will father kings, though he will never be king himself. Macbeth begins to question the sisters further, but they vanish into the air.

As Macbeth and Banquo discuss the curious prophecies, Ross and Angus approach. They greet Macbeth with accolades from King Duncan. Angus tells Macbeth that they are to escort him to the king. Ross says the king has conferred upon Macbeth the title of Thane of Cawdor. Macbeth asks how the title can be granted him, since Cawdor is still alive. Angus replies that the thane has confessed to treason—a capital offense—although Angus says he is unsure whether the thane overtly aligned himself with King Sweno, covertly aided the traitorous Macdonwald, or both.

Musing over the prophetic fulfillment, Macbeth silently rejoices over his success, but fears the murderous thoughts those same predictions have unearthed. Banquo calls attention to Macbeth's deep, contemplative brooding at which Macbeth regains his composure and apologizes to the thanes, bidding his new escorts to take him to the king.

EQUIVOCATION
Equivocation—or double interpretation—reigns in this scene. For example, the day is both foul and fair; the sisters are both physical and spiritual; their gender is both male and female; Macbeth is both Glamis and Cawdor; Banquo is both lesser and greater, unhappier and happier than Macbeth; the predictions of the sisters are both good and evil.

ACT 1, SCENE 4

King Duncan honors Macbeth and names Malcolm heir to the throne.

AT HIS NORTHERN stronghold in Forres, King Duncan is again with his two sons, Malcolm and Donalbain, the young thane Lennox and several attendants. The king asks whether or not the officers assigned to execute Cawdor have returned with news that they have completed their task. Malcolm, the most politically capable of the group, says that though the officers have not returned, he has spoken with a witness who said the execution has, indeed, been performed.

Malcolm goes on to say Cawdor confessed his treasons, implored the king's forgiveness and profoundly repented his actions before dying—making his death far more honorable than his life. Duncan responds that he trusted Cawdor implicitly, cautioning his sons that a man's face can belie his thoughts. Macbeth and Banquo enter. King Duncan first welcomes Macbeth, calling him a worthy kinsman. The king says he feels ungrateful for not doing more to reward Macbeth, whose accomplishments, he admits, were so many and so fast, he could not keep pace with them.

Macbeth responds that service to the king is its own reward. King Duncan assures him that he will personally oversee his success. The king then turns his attention to Banquo, promising to take his fortune to heart as well. Banquo responds graciously that any future achievements of his will be the result of the king's efforts.

King Duncan addresses his sons and the rest of the court, saying his happiness is so full, he weeps tears of joy. In front of the assembly of thanes, he announces his intent that Malcolm, his eldest son, be made heir to the throne, formally naming him Prince of Cumberland. The king vows to further reward his deserving nobles and bids all to follow him to Macbeth's home at Inverness to strengthen their mutual loyalties. Taking his leave, Macbeth tells Duncan that, as host, he will ride ahead to announce the good news of the king's visit to his wife.

In an aside, Macbeth considers Malcolm's appointment an obstacle in his own path to the throne. He requests the stars stop shining so that darkness can cover his murderous intent. Despite feeling ashamed enough to hope his actions are hidden from his conscience, he resolves to murder King Duncan. The pangs of this ambivalence will grow larger, the closer Macbeth comes to committing the murder. As Macbeth leaves, King Duncan commends his actions to Banquo, calling Macbeth a kinsman without peer.

CUMBERLAND
The title, Prince of Cumberland, was given to the King of Scotland's eldest son and heir-apparent. It was the Scottish equivalent to the historical French *Dauphin* and the modern-day British *Prince of Wales*. Cumberland county is in northwestern England on the border with Scotland. Since 1974, Cumberland has been a part of the new county of Cumbria.

ACT 1, SCENE 5

Lady Macbeth hears of Duncan's visit and plans to murder him that night.

AT HER CASTLE in Inverness, some 25 miles southwest of Forres, Lady Macbeth reads aloud a letter from her husband. We come upon her as she is partway through the letter, which recounts the predictions of the Weird Sisters. It does not mention King Duncan's visit, but does mention Macbeth's promotion and therefore must have been sent by messenger some time between Macbeth's greeting by the escorts and his audience with the king.

The letter goes on to speak of Macbeth's destined rule as king, addressing Lady Macbeth as "my dearest partner of greatness" and telling her—in the written equivalent of hushed tones—to keep this knowledge confidential. Putting the letter down, Lady Macbeth speaks as if to her husband. She affirms that he will be king, which was promised to him by both fate and spiritual forces. She tells him her fears that he is too kindhearted to do the ruthless deed that must be done. She bids him come quickly to her, so she can excise anything in his nature that would stand in the way of his coronation.

A servant enters with news that King Duncan is on his way to Inverness. Lady Macbeth is at first incredulous, saying that if this were true, then Macbeth would have forewarned them. The servant reaffirms the truth of his message, saying Macbeth is coming and a fast messenger outpaced him to Inverness. Lady Macbeth sends the servant to take care of the exhausted messenger, saying he brings great news.

Alone, Lady Macbeth utters a chilling soliloquy. Three times she invokes supernatural assistance: first from evil spirits to replace her feminity with cruelty; again from those same spirits to replace her milk with bitterness; and last from personified Night to cover her evil activities from heaven's view.

Macbeth enters and Lady Macbeth greets him in an echo of the Weird Sisters' triplet: Glamis, Cawdor and king hereafter. She tells him that his letter revealed the future so distinctly to her that she feels as if she is living in that future now.

Macbeth only says that Duncan is coming and expects to leave the next day. Lady Macbeth replies that that day will never come. After Macbeth reacts to her words, she cautions him to hide his feelings behind a welcoming countenance. She continues with a metaphor: look like a flower, but act like the snake beneath it. Taking charge, she tells him to "put this night's great business" into her hands. Macbeth leaves her, saying ambiguously, "We will speak further."

CONROL
From 1.5 until the night of the coronation banquet, Lady Macbeth will take the lead on the motivation, planning and management of her husband's ascendence. After the coronation banquet, however, her trajectory will sharply fall into madness, forcing Macbeth to undertake the grim task of securing his ill-gotten power.

ACT 1, SCENES 6 & 7

Duncan arrives at Inverness; Lady Macbeth bolsters Macbeth's resolve.

IN SHARP CONTRAST to the dark night ahead, King Duncan sees Macbeth's castle at Inverness and remarks to his entourage—his thanes and his sons—that it has a most delightful ambiance. Banquo replies that swallows favor the castle for their nests, a sure sign of sweet air. Lady Macbeth walks out to greet the king and the two share elaborate courtly courtesies. Lady Macbeth then escorts King Duncan to her husband.

Later that evening, outside the victory celebration in the great hall, Macbeth is plagued with doubts. In one of his most powerful soliloquies, he examines the finality of regicide, starting with the cold-hearted axiom: *if the murder would end at the killing of Duncan, then it would be best to kill him that night.* If acts like this were indeed final, he reasons, without immediate consequences in this life, then people would risk the deferred consequences in the afterlife. But, he continues, there are earthly consequences to these actions—Duncan's murder will merely provide motivation and instruction for ambitious underlings to kill Macbeth.

Macbeth voices his guilt at planning Duncan's murder, while being his trusted thane and host. He believes that Duncan has actually been a virtuous king and Macbeth imagines personified Pity, along with the angels of heaven, will announce the murder, causing a nationwide outpouring of grief. (The language hints at his fear of discovery as well.) Macbeth closes the soliloquy, saying he has no motivation to kill this man except his own overblown ambition.

Lady Macbeth enters and asks why Macbeth has left the festivities, telling him King Duncan has been calling for him. Macbeth answers that he will not murder Duncan, especially since the king has honored Macbeth for his recent heroics on the battlefield.

Lady Macbeth berates her husband, calling him a coward. Macbeth defends his manhood, claiming no one in Scotland is as masculine as he. Lady Macbeth scoffs, saying if Macbeth were truly a man, he would follow through on his word. In a horrific statement, she vows she would crush the skull of her nursing child if she gave her word on it.

Macbeth is stunned. He asks her what would happen should they fail. Lady Macbeth says she will simply get the guards drunk and blame them for the murder once it is discovered. Caught up in the spirit of the plan, Macbeth adds that they can use the guards' daggers for the murder and smear them with Duncan's blood. He resolves himself completely to the regicide and the two rejoin the celebration.

CHILDREN
Children do not fare well in Macbeth. In this scene, Macbeth imagines Pity as an infant trumpeting the news of Duncan's murder and Lady Macbeth speaks of cudgeling a suckling. Later, Fleance will witness his father's murder and Macduff's child will be slaughtered. Finally, Macbeth will see a bloody infant rising from the sisters' cauldron, telling him to fear no man born of woman.

ACT 2, SCENE 1

Macbeth speaks with Banquo; his bloody dagger hallucination.

RETURNING TO THEIR room after the party, Banquo speaks with his son, Fleance. Banquo asks how late it is and Fleance answers that it is well after midnight, since the moon has already set. Preparing for bed, Banquo hands his sword and personal articles to Fleance, commenting on the starless darkness of the night. (This echoes the requests of Macbeth in 1.4 and Lady Macbeth in 1.5 for darkness to cover the horrible crime they will soon commit.)

Banquo continues, saying he is tired but unable to sleep because of nightmares. In the darkness, Macbeth approaches with a servant, startling the edgy Banquo, who calls for his sword and demands Macbeth identify himself. Macbeth makes himself known and Banquo relaxes, saying the king was in high spirits when he went to his bedchamber. Banquo then hands Macbeth a diamond—a gift from King Duncan to Lady Macbeth for her generous hospitality. The necessity for Banquo to deliver the diamond emphasizes Macbeth's suspicious absence from the night's celebration.

Changing the subject, Banquo intimates that the previous night he dreamed of the Weird Sisters, who accurately predicted Macbeth's Cawdor promotion. Playacting, Macbeth says he hasn't thought of the sisters, but would be willing to discuss the significance of the predictions, if Banquo had the time. Banquo replies cordially and Macbeth, hoping Banquo will interpret his deeper meaning, says that Banquo will win favor, if he assists Macbeth in the future.

The grave, subversive meaning of this statement is not lost on Banquo, who replies that he will be happy to assist Macbeth in any way, so long as his loyalty to Duncan is not compromised. Knowing he may have gone too far, Macbeth agrees, lightheartedly bidding them good night.

As Banquo and Fleance retire for the night, Macbeth sends his servant to tell Lady Macbeth to ring the bell when his drink is ready. Many commentators feel this is a coded message, meaning: "Ring the bell when the guards have been drugged."

Alone and at a moment of unmitigated stress, Macbeth is startled by the vision of a dagger hovering before him. He grasps unsuccessfully for it as he follows it down the hallway toward Duncan's room and rationally deduces that it must be a hallucination. Transforming before Macbeth's eyes, the dagger becomes stained with clots of blood. He bids the floor to silence his criminal steps and then hears the bell ring. Whispering for Duncan to remain oblivious to his death knell, Macbeth goes to commit the murder.

ILLUSION
Macbeth presents the audience with a wide variety of illusory images. The Weird Sisters are indefinite in form, but real in nature. The dagger is definite in form, but Macbeth understands that it is a hallucination. Banquo's ghost is definite in form, but Macbeth is unable to deduce that it is unreal. Lastly, the apparitions are definite and real, but are illusory forms the spirits have assumed.

ACT 2, SCENE 2

Macbeth and his wife attend to the post-murder details.

ALONE WHILE HER husband commits the regicide, Lady Macbeth comments that while the alcohol has made the guards drunk, it has made her bold. She is startled by the shriek of an owl and surmises it is an omen that the king has just been killed. She says she has drugged the guards so heavily, it is hard to tell whether they are alive or dead. Macbeth calls out in confusion from the hallway and Lady Macbeth fears that the house has awakened before the king could be murdered.

Lady Macbeth says she left the daggers in a place where Macbeth could easily find them. She claims she would have murdered Duncan herself had he not reminded her of her sleeping father. Macbeth enters holding bloody daggers. A disjointed conversation follows. Macbeth reveals that the princes awakened, one laughing and the other crying, "Murder." Macbeth hid as they said their prayers and fell back to sleep. Distraught, he tells his wife he could not respond to their prayers with "Amen." Lady Macbeth advises him not to dwell on such things or it will make them insane.

Macbeth says he thought he heard a voice call out, "Sleep no more. Macbeth does murder sleep." Lady Macbeth becomes irritated at this. She tells her husband that he is weakening himself with such cowardly imaginings and directs him to wash the blood from his hands.

She asks him why he brought the daggers back from Duncan's room, reminding him that he was supposed to leave them behind. She demands he take the daggers back and smear blood on the guards. Macbeth refuses, afraid to face the reality of his crime. Lady Macbeth chastises him, telling him he is acting childishly. She takes the daggers from him, saying she will smear blood on the faces of the guards herself to make them appear guilty.

As his wife exits, a knock at the south entrance startles Macbeth. He looks at his bloody hands and says all the water in the ocean cannot possibly wash them clean. Lady Macbeth soon returns and points out that although her hands are now as blood-soaked as Macbeth's, she is not as cowardly.

At the sound of more knocking, Lady Macbeth urges her husband to retreat with her to their bedroom. There, she says, they can wash up and change into night clothes in case they are called for. Noticing Macbeth's distracted look, she tells him to not be so lost in his thoughts. Macbeth says he'd rather be in a daze than confront what he's done. As they exit, Macbeth laments that the knocking cannot wake Duncan.

SLEEP
Macbeth cries out after hearing a voice proclaim the end of sleep. Confused, Lady Macbeth thinks her husband is talking to someone who has awakened before he could commit the murder. Later, at the end of 3.4, we find Macbeth is having difficulty sleeping; in 5.1, we find Lady Macbeth is a troubled sleepwalker—more evidence that their guilt has placed them outside the natural order.

ACT 2, SCENE 3

Macduff discovers the murdered king; the princes flee for their safety.

AS THE KNOCKING persists, a porter stumbles onto the stage and slowly makes his way toward the door. In soliloquy, he pretends to be the doorman at the entrance to hell. With humor, he runs through a catalogue of possible new arrivals at hell's gates: a suicided farmer, an equivocating defendant, a thieving tailor. The porter then complains that Macbeth's castle is too cold for hell. After calling for patience to the person knocking and reminding them to tip the porter, he at last opens the door.

The two thanes, Macduff and Lennox, enter. Macduff complains about having to knock for so long. At Macduff's inquiry, the porter says he was carousing until three o'clock in the morning. He comically instructs Macduff on the three effects of alcohol: a red nose, sleepiness and the need to urinate. With a series of humorous metaphors, he goes on to claim that alcohol stirs the passions, but impedes performance. Playing the straight man, Macduff says that obviously alcohol did all these things to the porter last night. The porter agrees as Macbeth enters.

Macbeth exchanges greetings with the thanes. Macduff asks if the king has awakened. Finding that he has not, Macduff mentions that he was commanded by the king to wake him early. Macbeth escorts Macduff and Lennox to Duncan's chamber door. Macduff goes in to wake Duncan as Lennox and Macbeth converse outside the door. Lennox says that the night was bizarre—people heard screaming, voices predicting catastrophe and owls screeching. Some even felt earthquakes.

Macduff returns in horror, telling them the king has been murdered. Macbeth and Lennox go into the bedroom as Macduff shouts to wake the household. The alarm bell rings and Lady Macbeth enters, asking what the disturbance is about.

Banquo arrives and Macduff says the king has been murdered. Macbeth and Lennox return with Ross. Macbeth pretends to be distraught. The princes enter and Macbeth tells them in metaphor that their father has been murdered, intimating that they are suspects. Lennox says that apparently the guards killed the king and Macbeth feigns repentance at killing them in revenge. Macduff questions Macbeth's actions and Macbeth defends himself, saying he reacted out of love for Duncan. Lady Macbeth faints and is carried off. The thanes agree to dress and meet in the great hall to solve the crime.

Alone, the princes plan to flee Inverness. Malcolm says he will go to England. Donalbain, claiming it is safer to separate, says he will go to Ireland.

HARROWING
The porter scene—a comedic contrast to the bloody murder—parodies the Harrowing of Hell from medieval morality plays. In these plays, Christ is shown (after his crucifixion and before his resurrection) coming to the gates of hell to collect the redeemed sinners.

ACT 2, SCENE 4

Nature rebels against the regicide; Macbeth is to be crowned king.

THE FOLLOWING DAY, Ross and an old man stand outside the castle at Inverness, talking over the tragic events. The old man says that in his seventy years of life, he has seen many strange and terrible events, but the events of the past night have dwarfed them in significance. Ross proclaims that the heavens are judging the murder by shrouding the daylight in darkness. (Renaissance folklore integrally tied regicide with a subsequent backlash of natural processes.)

The old man agrees. He claims that a noble, high-flying falcon was attacked and killed by a lowly mouse-hunting owl—a symbol of inverted hierarchy. Ross continues the old man's motif, saying the well-bred horses in King Duncan's royal keep suddenly went wild, broke out of their stables and could not be controlled by their handlers. The old man adds that he heard those same horses now bite and tear at each other, to which Ross agrees, saying he was an eye witness to these unnatural occurrences.

Macduff enters, joining the two men in their conversation. With tongue in cheek, Ross asks him how the world is going now. Macduff scoffs, asking rhetorically if Ross cannot see for himself.

Ross asks Macduff if he knows who committed the horrible murder and Macduff answers cautiously that it must have been King Duncan's guards, calling them "those that Macbeth hath slain." Ross, catching hold of Macduff's skepticism, exclaims his horror at the act and then presses further, asking what the guards could possibly hope to gain from the murder.

Macduff, safely repeating the official report, says obviously the guards were hired to assassinate the king. He reminds them that the two princes, Malcolm and Donalbain, have already fled the country. This, he says, has made them the primary suspects in the crime.

Ross, bringing the conversation to its true point, asks Macduff if Macbeth is to be king in their absence. Macduff answers that the thanes have already chosen Macbeth, who is now on his way to Scone for the coronation. Ross asks if Macduff will attend the ceremony and the latter answers that he will instead travel to his home in Fife. Ross says that he will be going to Scone and Macduff expresses his hope that Macbeth's reign will not be worse than Duncan's. The men part as the old man utters a blessing.

SCONE
Scone, just north of Fife, is the traditional coronation site of Scottish kings. There, the king would be placed on the stone of destiny, fabled to be the stone Jacob slept on at Bethel. It's original inscription read: "If the destiny prove true, then the Scots are known to have been kings where'er men find this stone." The stone was moved to England in 1296 by Edward I and finally returned to Scotland in November 1996.

ACT 3, SCENE 1

Macbeth plans the murders of Banquo and Fleance.

INSIDE THE PALACE at Forres where Duncan ruled, Banquo considers Macbeth's newly-gained kingship and the prophecies of the Weird Sisters. He muses that Macbeth has acquired the throne and the thaneships of both Cawdor and Glamis, just as the sisters promised. He suspects Macbeth has acted wickedly to obtain his position. He realizes, however, the kingship will pass to his own progeny if what the sisters prophesied remains accurate.

Hearing the royal fanfare, Banquo ceases his reverie. Macbeth and Lady Macbeth enter as king and queen, along with an entourage which includes Ross and Lennox. In a grand gesture, Macbeth greets Banquo as his chief guest. Lady Macbeth agrees, saying the coronation banquet that evening would be incomplete if Banquo were not invited. Macbeth invites him formally and Banquo accepts, equally formally. Macbeth begins a series of questions which uncover Banquo's plans for the afternoon. He finds that Banquo will be riding until a couple of hours after sunset.

Macbeth admonishes him not to miss the banquet and Banquo replies that he will not. Changing the subject, Macbeth says the princes have fled to England and Ireland, where they tell lies and deny their crimes. He says they will discuss the situation more in tomorrow's council.

Macbeth then presses him for more information, asking if his son, Fleance, is riding with him. Banquo answers that he is and then says it is time for him to leave. Macbeth says farewell and turns to his other guests, telling them to bide their time until the banquet. He says he will be alone until then and everyone exits— including Lady Macbeth— except for Macbeth and a servant. Macbeth sends the servant to bring in the men who wait outside.

Macbeth, in soliloquy, expresses his fear of Banquo's integrity, wisdom and valor. Macbeth fears that all he has done in killing Duncan is to clear the way for Banquo's descendants. Wishing to change this future, he challenges fate to a deadly contest.

The servant brings in two men and then leaves. Macbeth tells the men that Banquo is responsible for all their troubles. The men agree. Macbeth goes on to say that it is improper for him to act in this situation, since he is king. The men say they will do it. Macbeth says they must kill Banquo and Fleance away from the palace and then ushers them into a room where they will await further instruction. In an aside, Macbeth says that if fate allows, Banquo's soul will be in heaven that night.

DISTANCE
Lady Macbeth is not present, nor is she seen masterminding or even influencing Macbeth in his plot to murder Banquo and Fleance. This marks the beginning of the growing distance that will characterize their once close relationship. That distance will culminate in the nihilistic eulogy Macbeth gives her after he hears of her death.

ACT 3, SCENES 2 & 3

Lady Macbeth speaks with her husband; the murder of Banquo.

LADY MACBETH SENDS a servant for her husband. Alone, she expresses her inability to enjoy their ill-gotten gain. When Macbeth enters, she chastises him for his depression and urges him not to dwell on what cannot be changed. Macbeth reminds her of their shared nightmares. He says he would rather be dead like Duncan than have to continue to endure mental torture and sleeplessness. He points out that they have done their worst to Duncan and nothing else can hurt the old king now.

At this, Lady Macbeth tells him to at least look cheerful for his guests. Macbeth agrees and counsels her to do the same. In a half-hearted attempt to shield his wife from the knowledge of his plan to murder Banquo, he asks her to be especially nice to Banquo at the banquet. The reason for this, Macbeth says, is because he now feels Banquo is dangerous. Macbeth rages that Banquo and Fleance are still alive. Lady Macbeth says they won't live forever. Her husband finds comfort in this and says before the night falls a dreadful deed will be done. He tells his wife to remain innocent to it saying more evil deeds will strengthen the evil they have already begun.

Outside the palace, the two murderers Macbeth hired to kill Banquo and Fleance enter in mid-conversation with a third. The third murderer says he was sent by Macbeth to join them. The second murderer tells his partner they can trust this man since he was given the same instructions they were. Convinced, the first murderer welcomes the newcomer and points out that since it is dusk, Banquo and Fleance will soon be approaching.

The third murderer hears horses. Offstage, Banquo calls for a torch. The second murderer whispers to the others that it must be Banquo since everyone else is in the palace. The third murderer says he hears Banquo handing the horses over to a servant. He points out that Banquo will walk from there to the palace—nearly a mile away—as is the general custom. Banquo and Fleance enter with a torch. Banquo stops. Looking up, he says that it will rain.

In response, the first murderer attacks him, saying, "Let it come down." Banquo frantically shouts for Fleance to run so he may one day avenge. Banquo dies as Fleance escapes to safety. The third murderer asks who put out the torch and the first says he thought that was the plan. The third murderer then says that, although they killed Banquo, they allowed his son to escape. The second says they bungled the most important part of their mission. The first murderer suggests they report what happened to Macbeth and they head back to the palace.

MISTRUST
The two murderers first debate whether they can trust the third—a man they do not know. Situations like this further the sense of mistrust, treason and betrayal in the play, even among men who are about to murder Banquo while his son watches.

ACT 3, SCENE 4

Macbeth sees the ghost of Banquo at the coronation banquet.

THE BANQUET IS SET and Macbeth enters with Lady Macbeth, Ross, Lennox and lords. Macbeth invites his guests to be seated according to their rank and then welcomes them all. His guests thank him and take their seats. Macbeth tells them that he will mingle first while the queen stays seated. From her seat, Lady Macbeth tells her husband to bid the guests welcome on her behalf, because she is delighted they have come.

Macbeth looks up and sees the murderer standing in the doorway, his face splattered with blood. Quickly excusing himself, Macbeth approaches the murderer and in a low voice asks if Banquo has been killed. The murderer answers that he cut Banquo's throat, though Fleance has escaped. Macbeth says, except for that, the murder would have been perfect. The murderer tells him Banquo lies in a ditch with twenty gashes in his head. Macbeth decides he can forget about the young Fleance for now and he dismisses the murderer. Lady Macbeth approaches and exhorts her husband to be a better host.

At this, Macbeth returns to his guests and offers a toast to their health. Lennox bids Macbeth to sit, but the ghost of Banquo enters and takes Macbeth's seat. Not yet seeing the apparition, Macbeth says he hopes Banquo is late out of forgetfulness rather than misadventure. Again Macbeth is urged to sit, but he says the table is full. Lennox, confused (because Macbeth is the only one who can see the ghost) points to where the ghost is seated and tells the king they have reserved that seat for him.

Macbeth points to Banquo's ghost, asking who has murdered him. The lords ask what he is talking about. Macbeth shouts defensively that he is not responsible and tells the ghost not to shake his bloody head at him. Ross says they should all go, because the king is not well. As they rise to depart, Lady Macbeth urges them to sit and enjoy themselves, saying her husband's fit will soon pass. She whispers to Macbeth that it is only another hallucination like the bloody dagger; the seat is empty. Macbeth confronts the ghost and it disappears. Macbeth makes another toast and the ghost returns. Macbeth screams at it to go away. Lady Macbeth tells the guests he is just sick. The ghost finally disappears. Macbeth begins to speak of his vision and Lady Macbeth quickly silences him as their guests leave.

Macbeth says he will send for the absent Macduff and go see the Weird Sisters to ask for their advice in the morning. He intimates he cannot turn from the murderous path he has chosen and they exit together.

ACCUSATION
After hearing the murderer's bloody description of the killing of Banquo, Macbeth subconsciously conjures up the image of the victim, complete with bloodied hair. The image accuses Macbeth, which is tantamount to Macbeth accusing himself.

ACT 3, SCENES 5 & 6

Hecate scolds the Weird Sisters; Macduff refuses Macbeth's summons.

ON THE HEATH, before a background of thunder and darkness, Hecate, goddess of the night, approaches the Weird Sisters. The first sister greets her and says she looks angry. Hecate answers that she has reason: the sisters have engaged in macabre riddles with Macbeth without involving her. Macbeth, she says, is undeserving of their assistance, since he loves only himself and shows no care for them. She instructs them to meet her at hell's river of sorrow in the morning.

There, she says, Macbeth will come to discover his destiny. She instructs the sisters to bring their cauldron, spells, charms and other implements. For her part, Hecate says she will take to the air to construct a dismal end for Macbeth. She will change a moondrop into magical spirits to trick Macbeth when he comes at midday. The result of her trickery will be to make Macbeth think he is greater than destiny, death and fear. Hecate reminds the sisters that the greatest enemy of humankind is fearlessness. She leaves to return to her attendant spirit as the sisters rush to complete their tasks.

At the palace in Forres, Lennox, in mid-conversation, tells a lord that their thinking is similar: strange things have been happening in the royal court. Speaking sarcastically, he points out several examples. First, he says, Macbeth pitied Duncan and then, suddenly, Duncan was dead. Second, Banquo went out walking too late at night and then he was dead. Whimsically, Lennox blames Fleance for his father's murder, since he fled just like Malcolm and Donalbain did after they supposedly had Duncan killed.

Continuing his sarcasm, Lennox says that surely Macbeth was right in killing the two guards, even though they were still drunk and asleep when he did so. Lennox says that the princes and Fleance would find out how terrible patricide is if Macbeth held them in his prison.

Changing the subject, Lennox asks the lord if he knows where Macduff is hiding since Macduff fell from Macbeth's favor by not attending the coronation banquet. The lord replies that Macduff has fled to England, where he plans to join Malcolm in asking for King Edward's assistance. Malcolm, he says, has been treated well by King Edward. Macduff hopes to form an alliance with Edward and Siward, lord of Northumberland, to restore Scotland to health. The lord says that Macbeth is furious at this and at Macduff's abrupt refusal of his summons to Forres. As they part, Lennox says he hopes Macduff is successful in ridding Scotland of its new tyrant to which the lord agrees.

HECATE
Many editors feel that Hecate's scenes were spurious additions made by Thomas Middleton in 1609. Their objections center on two main observations: Hecate adds nothing to the narrative action and she speaks a different verse form than the Weird Sisters. Neither objection is a definitive justification for this scene's omission.

ACT 4, SCENE 1

Macbeth witnesses the horrifying parade of apparitions.

THE THREE SISTERS gather at midday to await Macbeth's arrival. They toss pieces of animals into their boiling cauldron—toads, snakes, dogs, lizards, wolves, sharks, goats, tigers and human babies—as they chant. Hecate enters with three other witches. She commends the sisters for their painstaking obedience to her commands (in 3.5), promising they will all share in the rewards. Hecate leads everyone in a song, and they dance around the cauldron before she and her witches leave.

The second sister senses the arrival of someone evil and she commands the door to open for whoever knocks. It is, of course, Macbeth and he asks the Weird sisters what they are doing. They answer darkly that there is no word for what they do. Macbeth demands that they answer a question, even if it causes the natural world to unravel. They reply quickly that they will, but ask Macbeth if he would rather hear the answer from them or from their masters. Macbeth tells them to call their masters. Delighted, the sisters pour in more obscene ingredients and speak incantatory verse.

As they chant, a head wearing a war helmet rises out of the cauldron. Macbeth begins to speak to it, but the first sister silences him, saying it knows his thoughts. The head speaks, warning Macbeth to beware Macduff, then descends.

A second apparition rises: a baby covered in blood. It speaks to Macbeth, telling him to laugh, for no one born of woman will ever harm him. Again, the apparition descends. Macbeth calls out, saying because of this, he does not fear Macduff anymore, but will kill him anyway to ensure his own safety.

A third apparition comes forth: a crowned child holding a tree. It tells Macbeth that he will never be defeated until Birnam Wood marches against him at Dunsinane Hill. As the third apparition descends, Macbeth says this will never happen, since forests cannot be commanded to uproot and fight. Macbeth asks the sisters if Banquo's sons will reign in Scotland. The sisters warn him not to inquire, but he persists. The cauldron sinks and the sisters call forth a procession of eight kings, each resembling Banquo, the last of whom carries a mirror. The blood-soaked Banquo appears, pointing at the kings and smiling at Macbeth. The sisters dance then vanish with the kings.

Lennox enters from outside. He brings word of Macduff's flight to England. Enraged at the news, Macbeth resolves to seize Macduff's castle at Fife, vowing to kill his wife, his children and all his servants.

LINEAGE
Modern scholars now believe Banquo to be a mythic figure. Shakespeare's source, however, stated that Banquo was the patriarch of the Stuart dynasty— the line from which King James descended. The mirror in the eighth king's hand was originally intended to show King James his own reflection.

ACT 4, SCENE 2

The murder of Macduff's wife and son at their home in Fife.

AT THE MACDUFF castle in Fife, Ross speaks with Lady Macduff and her son. Frustrated, Lady Macduff asks Ross why her husband has fled Scotland. Ross answers that she must have patience. She retorts that her husband had none, adding that his fear has made him appear guilty, even if he was innocent. Playing the optimist, Ross offers that Macduff may have been wise, rather than fearful to which Lady Macduff scoffs, saying even animals don't abandon their loved ones.

Ross defends Macduff's honor, calling him noble, wise and fair. He tells Lady Macduff the times they are now living in are dangerous and unstable. Ross then says goodbye. Lady Macduff points angrily at her son and says he is fatherless, though his father lives. Restraining another defense of Macduff, Ross says it would be foolish for him to stay longer and rides off. Lady Macduff then turns to her son and they share a dark conversation that alternates between the serious and the humorous. She first asks him how he plans to live, since his father will never return. He answers he will live as the birds do, scavenging for whatever he can get.

Continuing her son's metaphor, Lady Macduff asks if he doesn't fear bird traps. He replies that no one sets traps for little birds like him. Turning serious, he says his father isn't dead, despite what she says. Lady Macduff says unswervingly that his father is dead and she asks him what he will do to replace him. He answers that a better question is what she plans to do to replace him. She quips that husbands are easily available at the market to which he replies that she'll be buying just to sell again (when his father returns).

The boy asks his mother if his father is indeed a traitor. She answers that he is, since he professed an oath and then broke it (meaning, he swore to love and protect his family and then abandoned them). He asks her what must be done with traitors and she answers they must be hanged by honest men. Trying to make light of this, the boy says surely there are enough liars to overpower the honest men and hang them. She laughs and he says he knows his father is not dead, because if he were, she would be weeping.

A messenger comes. He tells them they must leave, since they are in grave danger and then rides off. Two murderers enter and ask where the traitorous Macduff is hiding. The boys defends his father, saying he is not a traitor and the murderer stabs him without hesitation. The scene closes as Lady Macduff runs away screaming, pursued by the murderers.

TAINT
This scene places the reputation of Macduff in question: why would a good man abandon his wife and son at a time when they are most vulnerable? By tainting the integrity of Macduff, Shakespeare allows our estimation of him to waver, setting us up for the next scene, in which Malcolm cleverly tests Macduff's loyalty.

ACT 4, SCENE 3

Malcolm tests Macduff's loyalty; Ross tells Macduff of his family's murder.

MALCOLM AND MACDUFF ride near the palace of Edward the Confessor. Malcolm says they should weep for Scotland; Macduff counters that it is better to fight like men, since each day enough tragedies occur in Scotland to make heaven weep. Malcolm says he will do what is possible only when it is expedient. Questioning Macduff's intentions, he points out that Macduff would gain Macbeth's favor by betraying Malcolm—likening it to sacrificing a lamb to appease a god.

Macduff answers tersely that he is not treacherous. Malcolm points out that even those appearing good—like Macbeth himself—can actually be evil. Macduff says if Malcolm will not fight, then he has lost hope. Malcolm says perhaps Macduff lost his hopes in him where Malcolm first found his doubts in Macduff—the time he first heard Macduff had abandoned his loving family, leaving them vulnerable. Overcome, Macduff bewails Scotland's plight: good men will not fight her tyrants. Malcolm tells Macduff not to take offense, saying he does not completely mistrust Macduff.

Malcolm then reveals that Edward the Confessor, King of England, has offered ten thousand men to fight on Malcolm's behalf. He admits, however, that once he defeats Macbeth, Scotland will suffer more under his reign. Macduff is confused by Malcolm's statement, so Malcolm clarifies, saying he possesses an insatiable lust and greed. Macduff says that while these are dangerous vices, they can be accommodated in a king, so long as they are balanced by other virtues. Malcolm admits he has no virtues and claims that if he were king, he would wreak havoc on the earth.

Macduff grieves at this news. Malcolm asks if Macduff believes now that he is unfit to govern. Macduff scoffs, saying Malcolm is unfit to live, let alone govern.

Malcolm is pleased with Macduff's answer and he tells the thane he was only testing his integrity. He goes on to say that he is a virgin and has never wanted even the things he himself already owns. Macduff says now he doesn't know what to believe.

A doctor passes by, saying Edward the Confessor is coming after he cures his people. Malcolm explains to Macduff that Edward hangs a gold coin on the sick person's neck, prays for him and the person is miraculously healed. Ross rides up to join them and says Macbeth is battling uprisings in Scotland. After a long avoidance of the subject, he delivers the news to Macduff of his family's slaughter. Malcolm tells Macduff to turn his grief into revenge and eventually Macduff agrees. The three men ride to see King Edward.

BARREN
Malcolm suggests Macduff convert his grief for his family's murder into revenge. Macduff answers that Macbeth has no children, meaning there is no *quid pro quo* for his family's slaughter, since he cannot reciprocally murder Macbeth's descendants. In the play, Macbeth is portrayed as barren in contrast to Banquo's fertility—demonstrated earlier in the procession of kings conjured by the Weird Sisters.

ACT 5, SCENE 1

Lady Macbeth is seen sleepwalking while speaking of the murders.

MACBETH HAS MOVED to a castle in Dunsinane, eastern Scotland, just north of Fife where Macduff's family was murdered. A doctor and gentlewoman discuss Lady Macbeth's sleepwalking. The gentlewoman tells the doctor that since Macbeth has taken arms against uprisings in the country, she has seen Lady Macbeth rise in her sleep, write a letter, seal it and return to her bed. The gentlewoman refuses to repeat the things the queen says, because she has no witness to corroborate her story.

As they are talking, Lady Macbeth walks past, holding a candle. The gentlewoman confides that the queen has ordered a light be kept continually burning by her. They watch as Lady Macbeth first rubs her hands in a washing motion, then says, "Out, damned spot. Out I say!" She babbles a string of disjointed sentences about the murder, sometimes speaking as if to her husband, including the incriminating, "Yet who would have thought the old man to have had so much blood in him." She continues her sleep babble, speaking of Macduff's wife and obsessing over her hands—bloody, in her imagination—which she cannot wash clean.

Still in her sleep, Lady Macbeth speaks of Lady Macduff in rhyme: "The Thane of Fife had a wife. Where is she now?" (The similarity here to the cadence of Ophelia's madness in *Hamlet* is worth noting.) She continues obsessing over her hands—bloody, in her imagination—which she cannot wash clean. The doctor tells the gentlewoman it is not right for her to hear these things; she counters that it is not right for the queen to say them.

Lady Macbeth mourns that all the perfume in Arabia could not remove the smell of blood from her hands. The gentlewoman remarks that she would not trade places with the Lady Macbeth, even if it meant she could be queen.

The doctor confesses more than once that Lady Macbeth's disease is beyond his cure. Lady Macbeth speaks of Banquo in her sleep, assuring her imaginary listener that Banquo cannot return from the grave. Replaying the murder in her mind, she then returns to her bed, after imagining someone knocking at the gate. The doctor asks if she will sleep the rest of the night and the gentlewoman answers that she will.

The doctor says that mentally-troubled people will often tell their secrets in their sleep. He confides that Lady Macbeth is more in need of God's help, than a doctor's. He directs the gentlewoman to remove all the potential harms from the queen's bedside. He leaves, saying he dares not speak his thoughts.

SLEEP
Lady Macbeth's troubled slumber echoes Macbeth's worry that he has, indeed, murdered sleep, as the voices pronounced the night of the regicide. Other examples of this include the princes awakening at the instant of the murder and Macbeth's own insomnia.

ACT 5, SCENES 2 & 3

More thanes join Malcolm's army; Macbeth prepares for battle.

OUT IN THE countryside near Dunsinane, defecting thanes Menteith, Angus, Caithness and Lennox—hear the drums of the approaching English army. Menteith says the army is led by Malcolm, his uncle Siward and their fellow thane Macduff. Angus suggests they meet up with them in Birnam Forest. Caithness asks if Donalbain is with them. Lennox answers that he has seen a list of the gentry with them and Donalbain was not mentioned, although Siward's son was.

Menteith then asks what Macbeth's response was to the news of the approaching army. Caithness answers that Macbeth has fortified his castle at Dunsinane. He points out that some describe Macbeth as mad, while those who hate him less say he is acting with bravery. Angus adds that in either case Macbeth is now receiving the fruits of his evil deeds. Those with Macbeth, he says, obey him out of duty and not love. He describes Macbeth as a dwarf in a giant's robe. The thanes then ride off to join Malcolm's army in the fight against Macbeth.

Back in his castle at Dunsinane, Macbeth, in the presence of the doctor, yells at his attendants. Macbeth orders them not to bring any more reports, saying he doesn't care if every thane deserts him—he won't fear any man born of woman, as the spirits foretold. A frightened servant enters and, after being berated by Macbeth for his cowardice, proclaims the English army is approaching, ten thousand strong.

Sending him away, Macbeth calls for Seyton, his attendant. Speaking more to himself, he says this battle will be either his glory or his undoing. Dejected, he says he has lived long enough. Since he will never see fruits of a good life—honor, love, or friendship that should come with age—he wishes his life would end.

Seyton enters and Macbeth tells him to bring his royal armor. Seyton says Macbeth does not need it yet, but Macbeth says he will put it on anyway. He tells Seyton to send out more cavalry to search the countryside and hang anyone spreading fear. Turning to the doctor, Macbeth asks about the queen. The doctor replies she is not sick, but troubled in her sleep. Macbeth orders him to give her some drug to take away her sorrowful memories, but the doctor says she must cure herself.

While putting on his armor, Macbeth scoffs, saying medicine is useless. He asks the doctor if he can diagnose Scotland's troubles, since his thanes are deserting and the English are coming. Irritated, Macbeth removes his armor and exits, saying he will not fear until Birnam Forest marches to Dunsinane.

SEYTON
The pun on his armor-bearer's name (Seyton-Satan) is extended by the war gear dressing to include a pun on St. Paul's exhortation to "put on the whole armor of God. (Eph. 6:11 KJV)" Here Macbeth is obsessively putting on the whole armor of Satan. This pun would not have been missed by Shakespeare's audience, including of course, King James.

ACT 5, SCENES 4-6

The army marches to Dunsinane carrying boughs from Birnam forest.

NEAR BIRNAM FOREST, Malcolm, Macduff, Siward and his son meet up with the deserting thanes. With resonances to his father's murder, Malcolm says that he hopes the day will soon come when it is safe to sleep in one's bedchamber. Siward asks what the name of the forest is ahead of them and Menteith replies that it is Birnam Wood. Malcolm, setting in motion the fulfillment of the third apparition, tells the soldiers to carry branches to hide their number from Macbeth's scouts.

Calling Macbeth "the confidant tyrant," Siward reports that Macbeth has fortified Dunsinane for their ensuing siege. Malcolm claims it is Macbeth's last hope, since every thane who had opportunity has deserted him and only mercenary soldiers comprise his army (echoing Macdonwald's forces in 1.2). Macduff says not to underestimate Macbeth, but judge the battle after it is over. Siward agrees, saying that the time for decisions is fast approaching. He says that idle speculation only conveys hope, whereas decisions such as they speak of can only be settled on the battlefield.

Back at the castle in Dunsinane, Macbeth directs his soldiers to hang the banners on the outer walls. He tells them the castle is strong enough to withstand their siege, saying Malcolm's army will die of famine and disease before they penetrate its walls. Macbeth says he regrets so many deserters fortified their ranks, otherwise his army would have met them outside, man to man.

Macbeth asks what noise he hears and Seyton replies it is the cries of their women. Macbeth says he is numb to shrieks and cries now, although there was a time when it would have stood his hair on end. Macbeth asks Seyton what is the reason for their wailing and Seyton answers that the queen is dead.

In a strangely moving soliloquy—strange due mostly to its intensely nihilistic, bankrupt emotionality—Macbeth offers a benediction of hopelessness. He describes life in famous terms: we are all actors who strut and worry on the stage for a short span. He calls it a tale told by an idiot, full of noise and energy, but in the end without meaning.

A servant comes in and tells Macbeth that the forest is moving toward the castle. Outside, the trumpets of the army are heard. Malcolm orders the soldiers to throw down their branches and let themselves be seen. He tells Siward and his son to lead the soldiers into battle. Malcolm and Macduff take an alternate course as the battle begins.

UNNATURAL
Macbeth disbelieves the servant who tells him of the forest's advance against the castle—the fulfillment of the third apparition's unnatural precondition for his defeat. With the movement of the forest complete, the only remaining unnatural event is for Macbeth to be slain by a man not born of woman.

ACT 5, SCENE 7

Malcolm's army takes the castle at Dunsinane; Macduff kills Macbeth.

THE BATTLE RAGING around him, Macbeth claims he has been tied to a stake—like a bear in the medieval amusement of bear-baiting, in which small dogs attacked a tied bear. He takes heart, however, in the second apparition's pronouncement to fear no man born of woman. Siward's son arrives and challenges Macbeth. Young Siward says his sword will prove Macbeth is not to be feared. They fight, Siward's son is killed and Macbeth exits, saying he'll not fear a man born of woman.

To that setup, Macduff enters and looks around for Macbeth. In soliloquy, he confesses his wife and children's ghosts will continue to haunt him if Macbeth is slain by any soldier other than himself. He voices his disdain at having to fight petty mercenaries who only have a monetary stake in the outcome of the battle and he vows to sheath his sword, unused, if he cannot fight Macbeth. He hears a noise which sounds to him like a person of high rank is being announced and leaves to search for Macbeth in that general direction after invoking Fortune's assistance.

Malcolm and Siward enter next. Siward reports that the castle has all but surrendered without much bloodshed. He goes on to say many of Macbeth's men have fought only until they had opportunity to switch allegiances. Malcolm repeats that thought with phrasing that doubles as, "We are fighting those who deliberately miss us with their swords" and "We are fighting those who eventually fight on our side." They both leave to go inside the nearly-surrendered castle.

Macbeth reenters in what some editors delineate Act 5, Scene 8. He asks rhetorically why he should play the Roman and die on his sword when he would rather use it on his enemies. Macduff enters and shouts for Macbeth to turn and face him. Macbeth says for Macduff to go away, since Macbeth already has his family's blood on his hands (this can be played as a taunt or a sincere warning). They begin to fight and Macbeth says he leads a charmed life in which no man born of woman can harm him. Macduff reveals he was born by Cesarean section (untimely ripped). He tells Macbeth to surrender, but though Macbeth is now fearful, he refuses and they leave the stage fighting.

Malcolm and Siward reenter with Ross, who tells Siward his son has been killed in battle. Siward asks if his wounds were in front and then says that is a high honor worth dying for. Macduff returns with Macbeth's head on a pole and leads everyone to cheer Malcolm as King of Scotland. Malcolm honors his noblemen, inviting them to his coronation at Scone.

DESTINY
Macbeth and Lady Macbeth are eulogized as "this dead butcher and his fiendlike queen." We find that the ambitious Lady Macbeth, ironically took her own life. Macbeth, who at first embraced his destiny and who later attempted to extinguish its fulfillment, comes to his fateful end as foretold by the first and second apparitions.

APPENDIX A: DRAMATIC MAPS

The Dramatic Maps that follow are schematic representations of *Macbeth* by scene. In each case, the main ideas of the scene are highlighted on the timeline, alongside their initial corresponding line number. The brackets attempt larger groupings of the ideas to provide a sense of the overall movement of the scene. The line numbers of Shakespeare's *Macbeth* differ greatly between Quartos, Folios and consequently, publishers—each publishing is an interpretive work. Keep in mind they are guidelines for general assistance; your specific version may vary.

1.1

The Weird Sisters plot

- line 1 — Three prophetic hags—the Weird Sisters—decide they will gather after the battle is over to meet with Macbeth in an open wasteland.

- 9 — Each sister responds to the call of her familiar and exits.

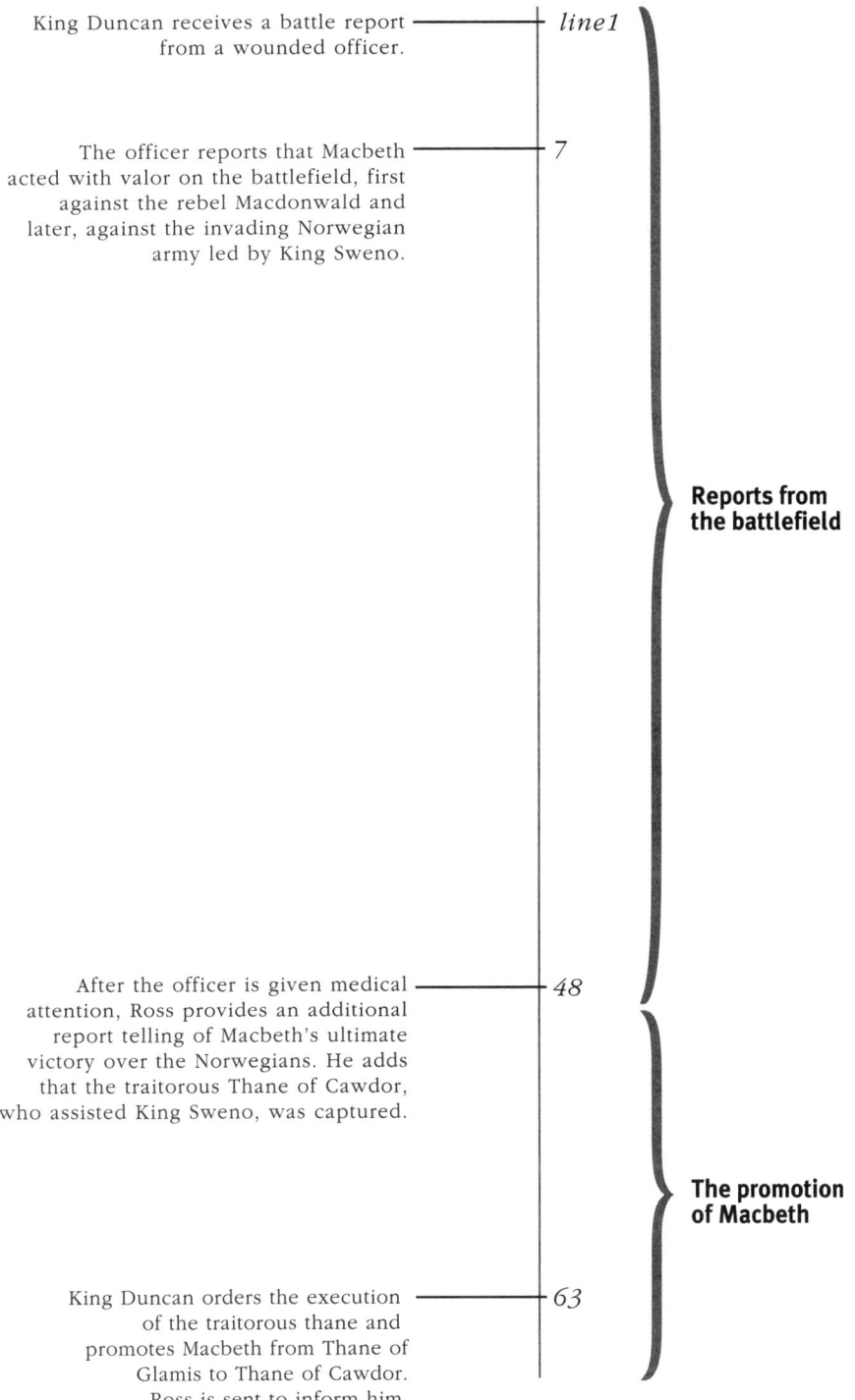

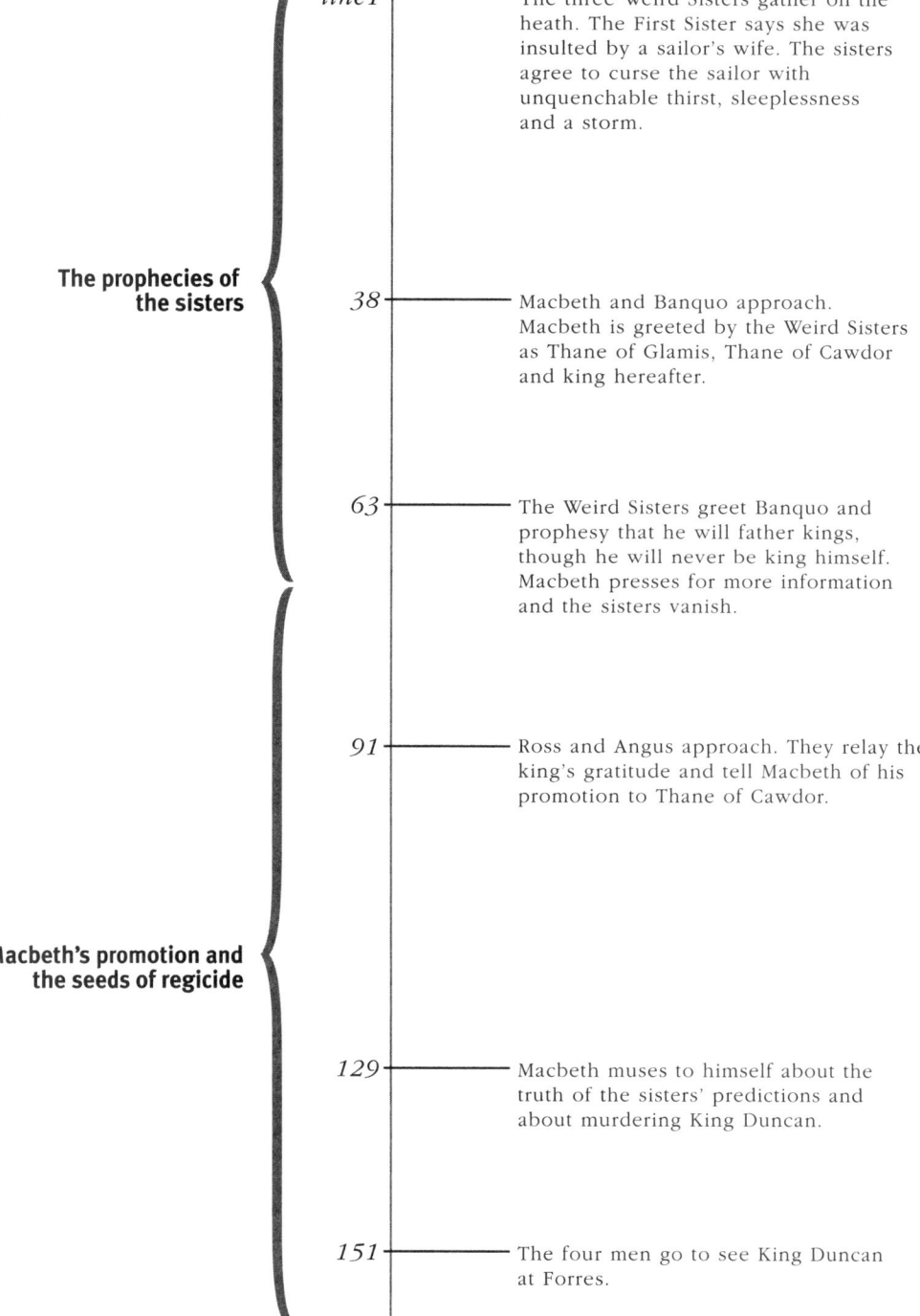

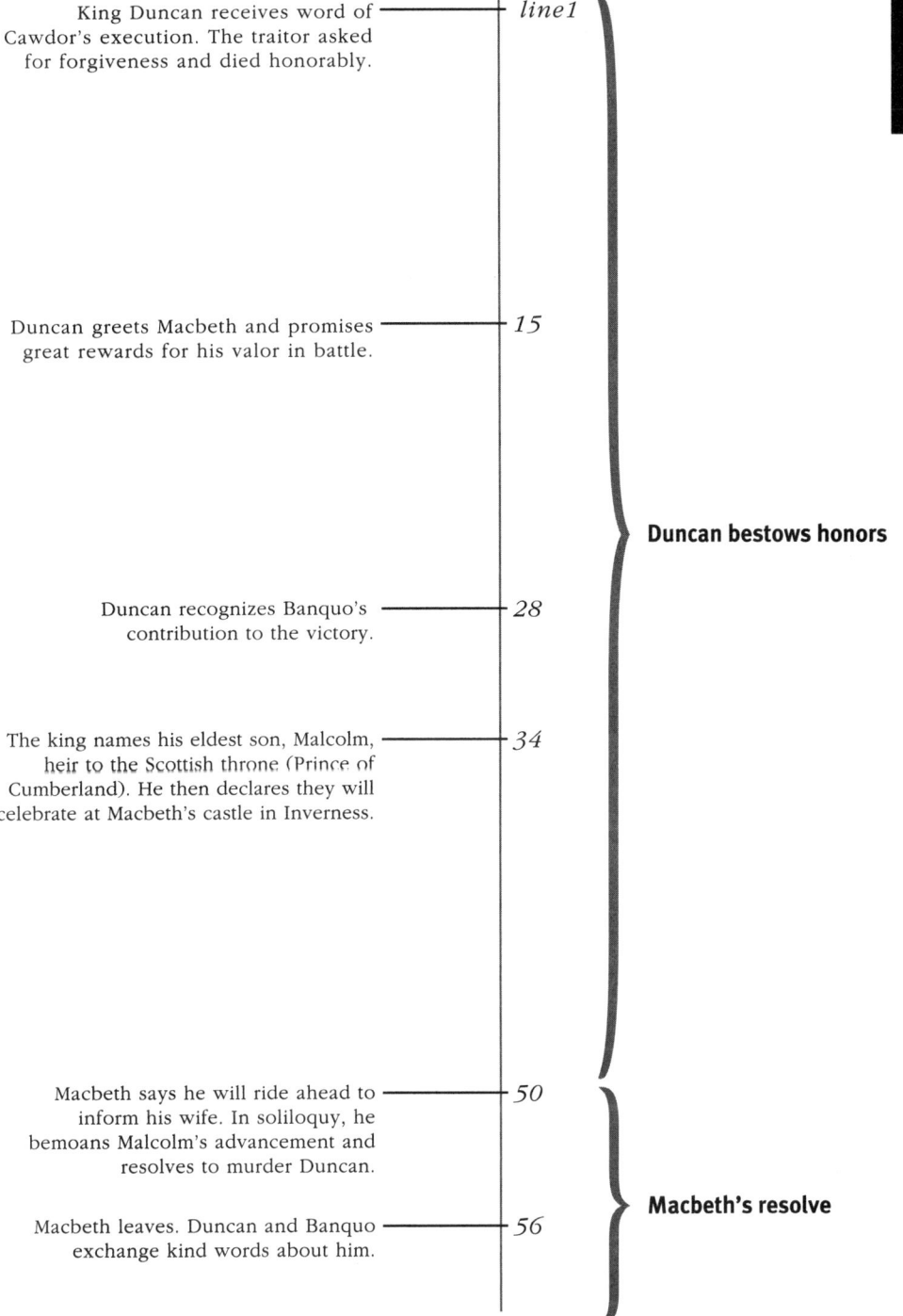

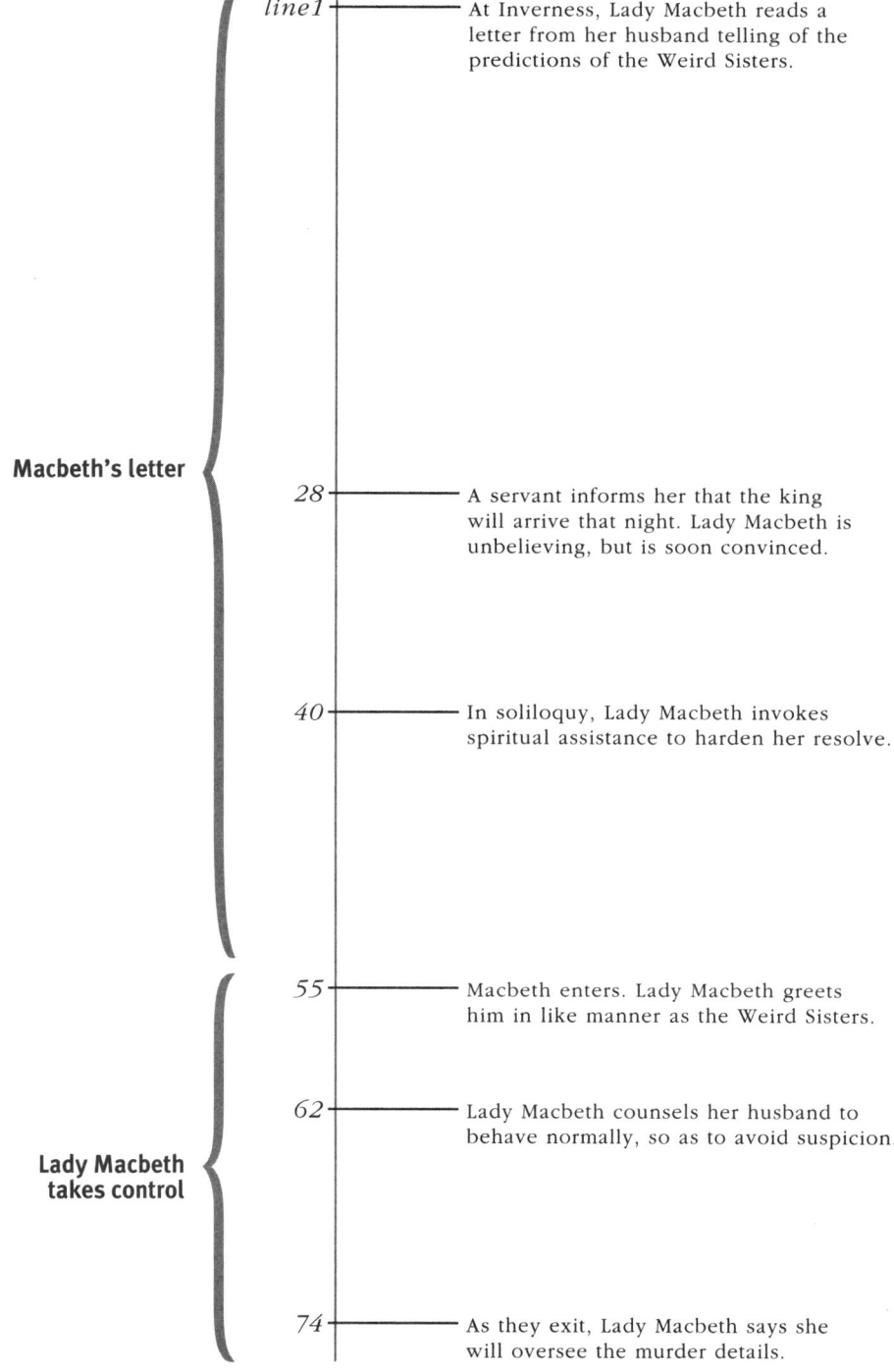

1.6

The king arrives

- *line 1* — King Duncan and his entourage arrive at Inverness. The king and Banquo comment on its pleasant ambiance.
- *14* — Lady Macbeth greets the king. They exchange elaborate courtly courtesies.
- *28* — King Duncan and Lady Macbeth.

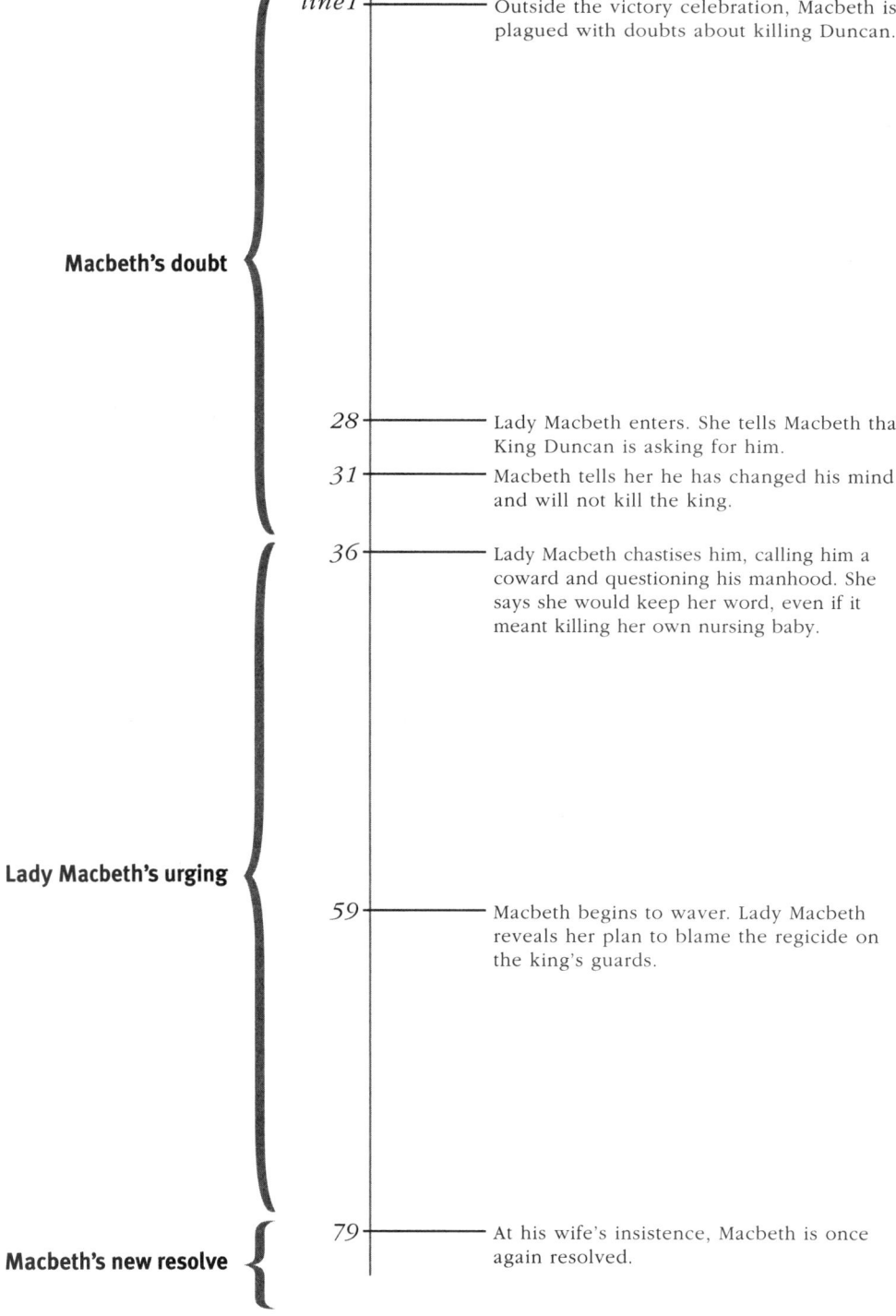

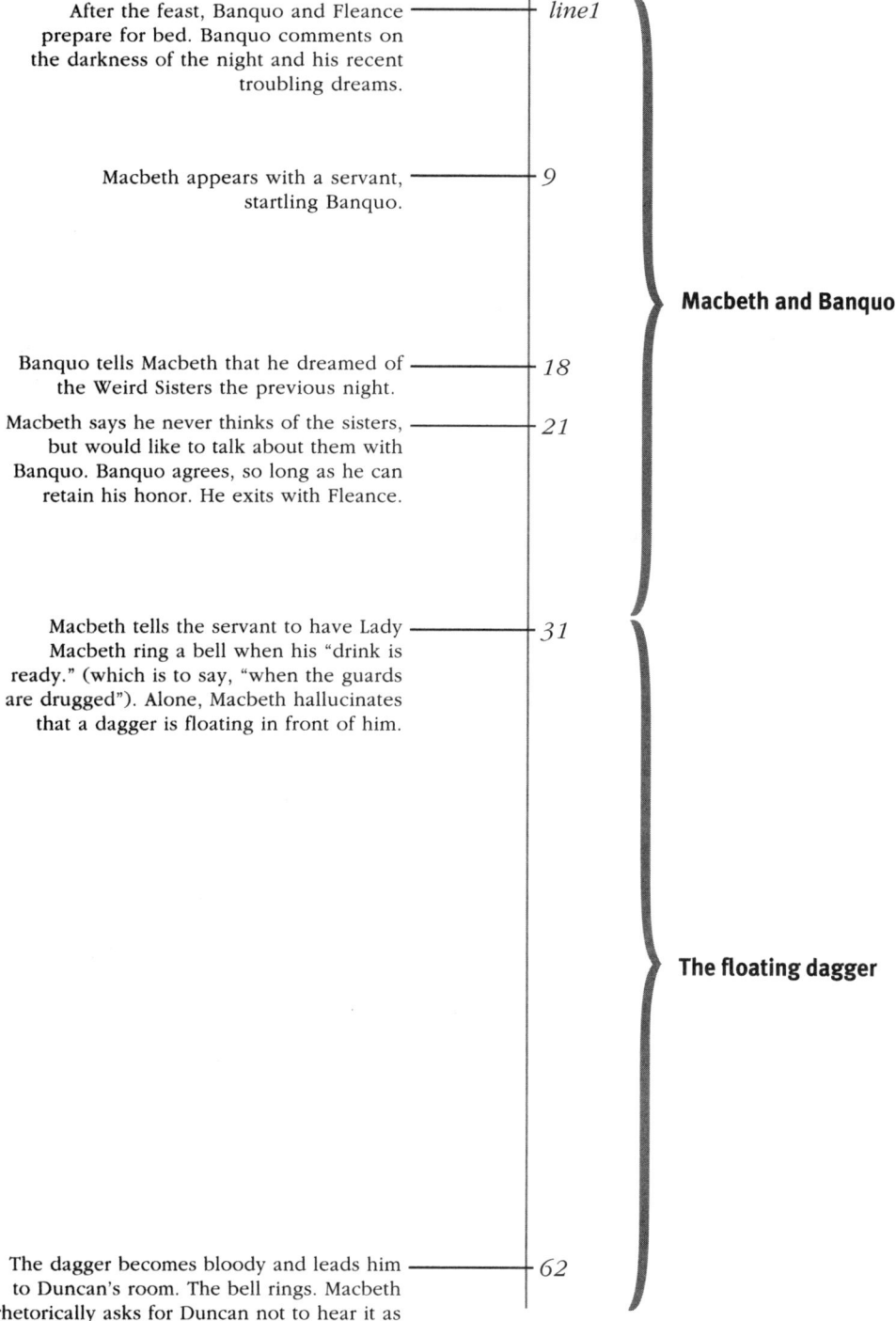

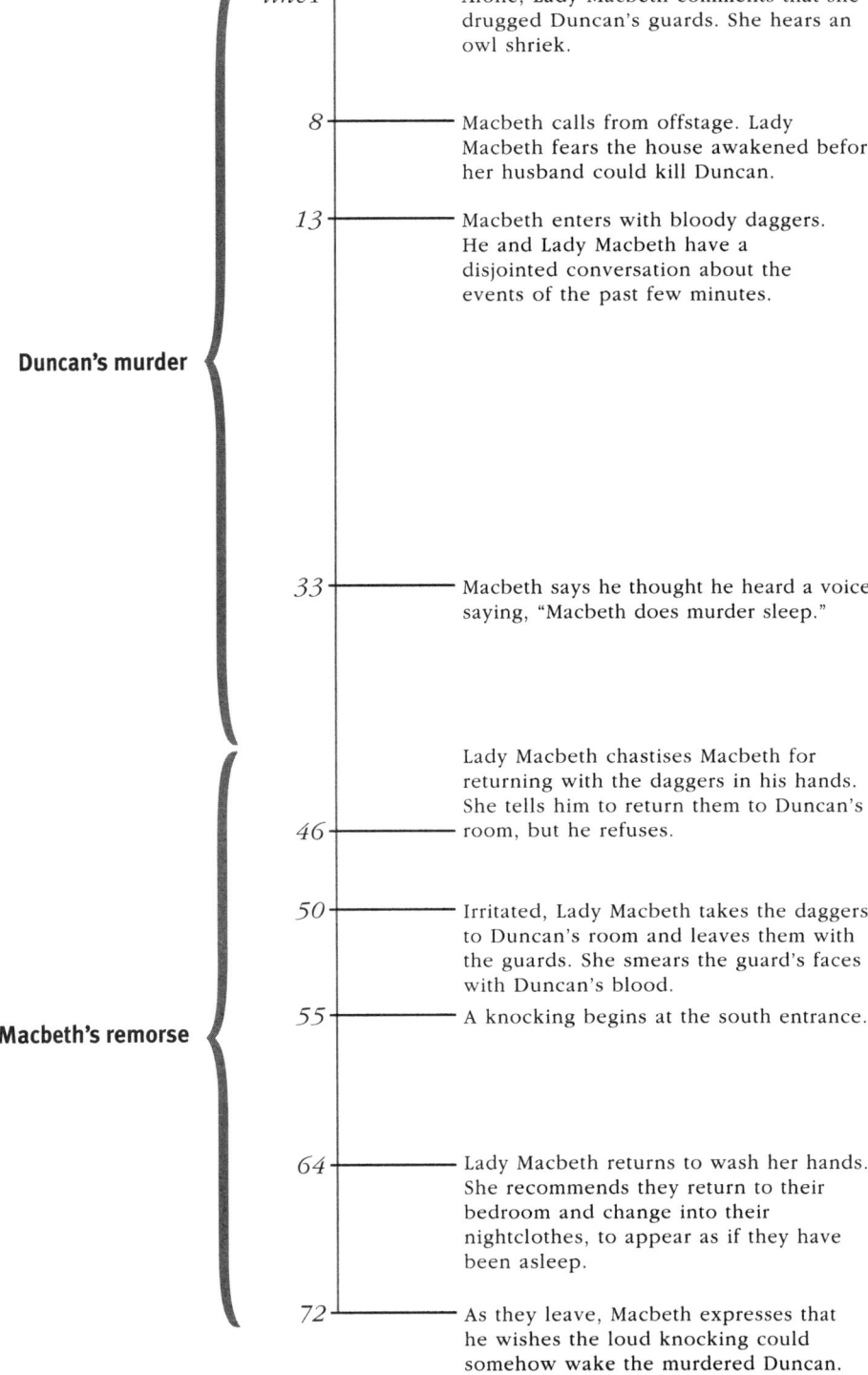

2.3

As the knocking continues, the drunken porter awakens and playacts he is the doorman to hell. — *line 1*

Macduff and Lennox are finally admitted to the castle. They have a comic discussion with the porter about the effects of drinking. — *19*

Macbeth enters and informs them the king is not yet awake. He escorts the thanes to Duncan's room. — *38*

Macduff goes in to wake Duncan, while Lennox talks with Macbeth about the eerie events of the previous night. — *47*

Macduff reenters horrified. He exclaims that King Duncan is dead and yells for the alarm to be sounded. Macbeth and Lennox run inside Duncan's room to confirm the news (while inside, Macbeth will kill the guards). — *58*

} **The regicide is discovered**

Lady Macbeth enters. Banquo enters and is told the news. Lady Macbeth feigns shock. — *76*

Macbeth and Lennox reenter. Macbeth feigns grief. Malcolm and Donalbain enter and are told their father has been murdered. Macbeth justifies his killing of Duncan's guards. — *86*

} **The reaction of the guests**

Banquo states his intention to investigate the murder of the king. The other thanes present, including Macbeth, agree. — *125*

Alone, Malcolm and Donalbain agree to flee for their safety: Malcolm to England and Donalbain to Ireland. — *131*

} **The flight of the princes**

DRAMATIC MAPS | 2.2 & 2.3 | 163

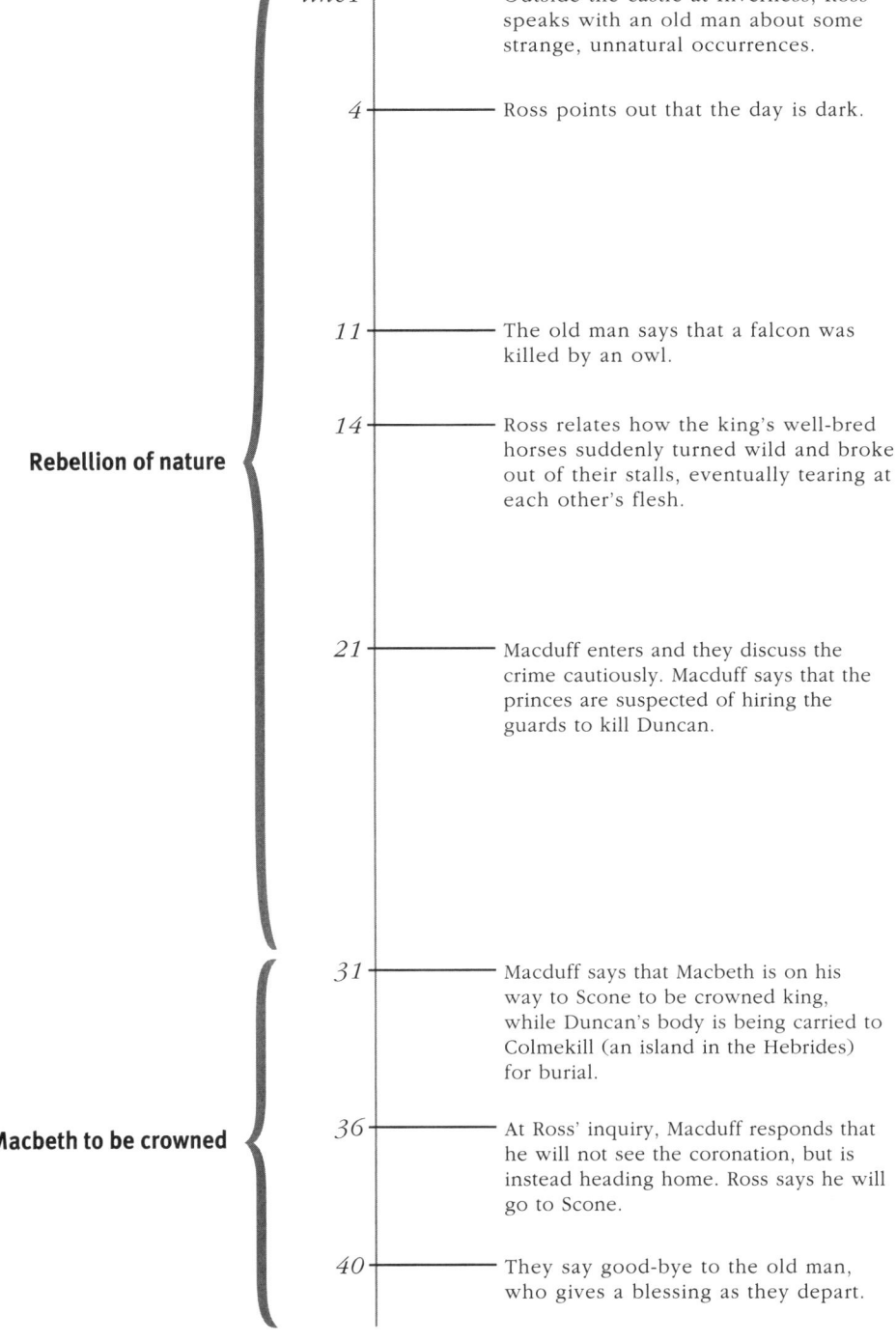

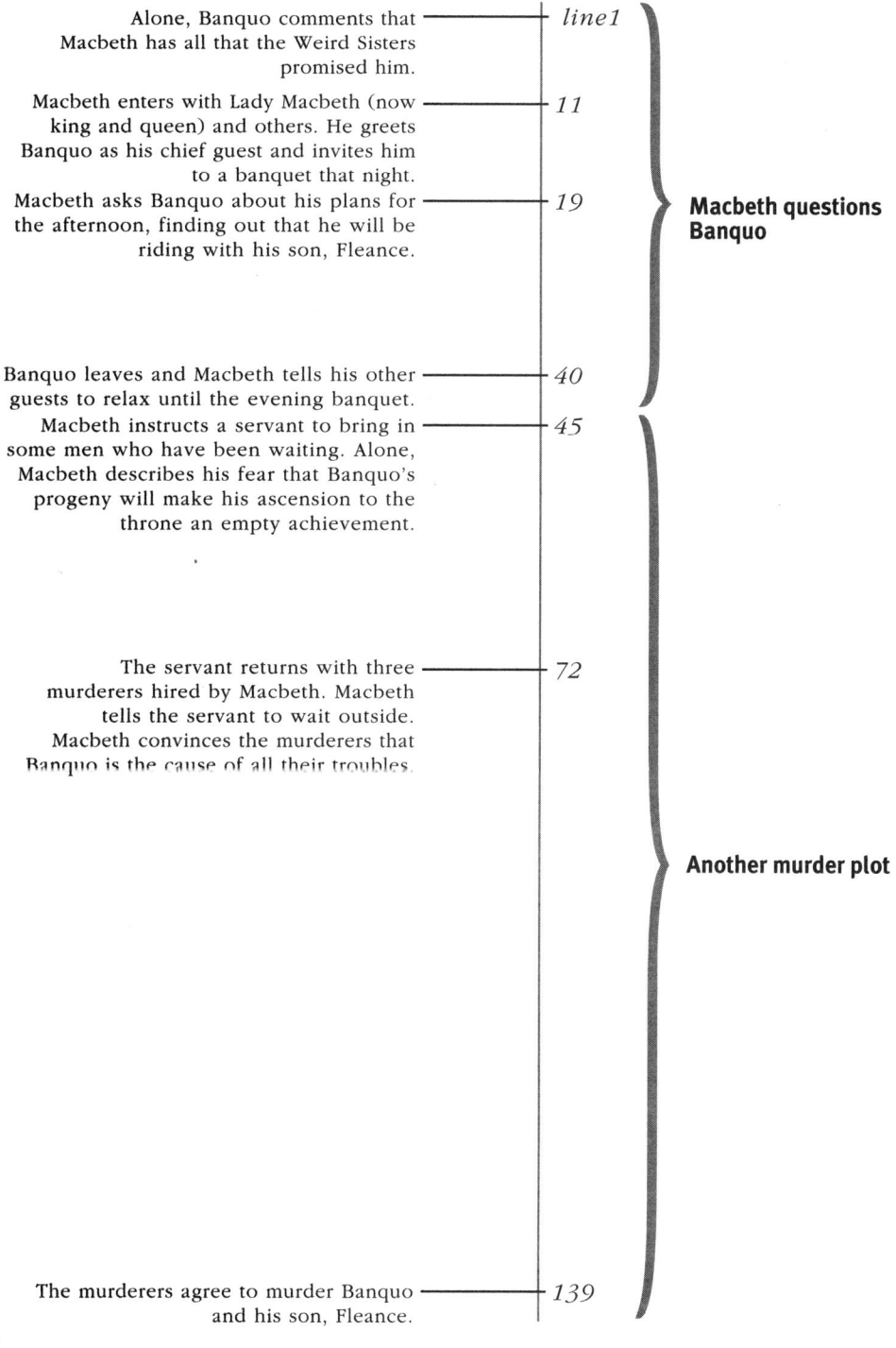

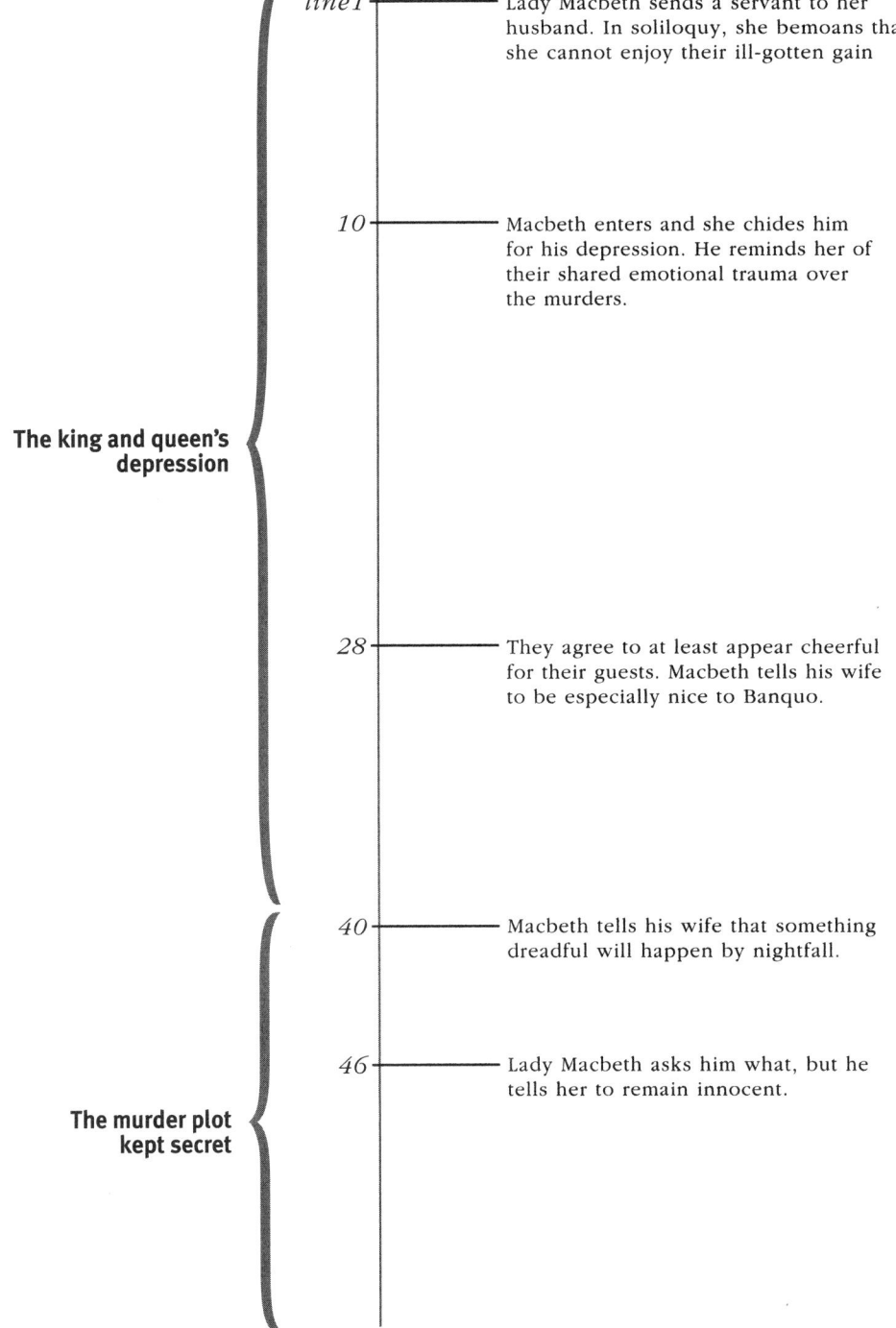

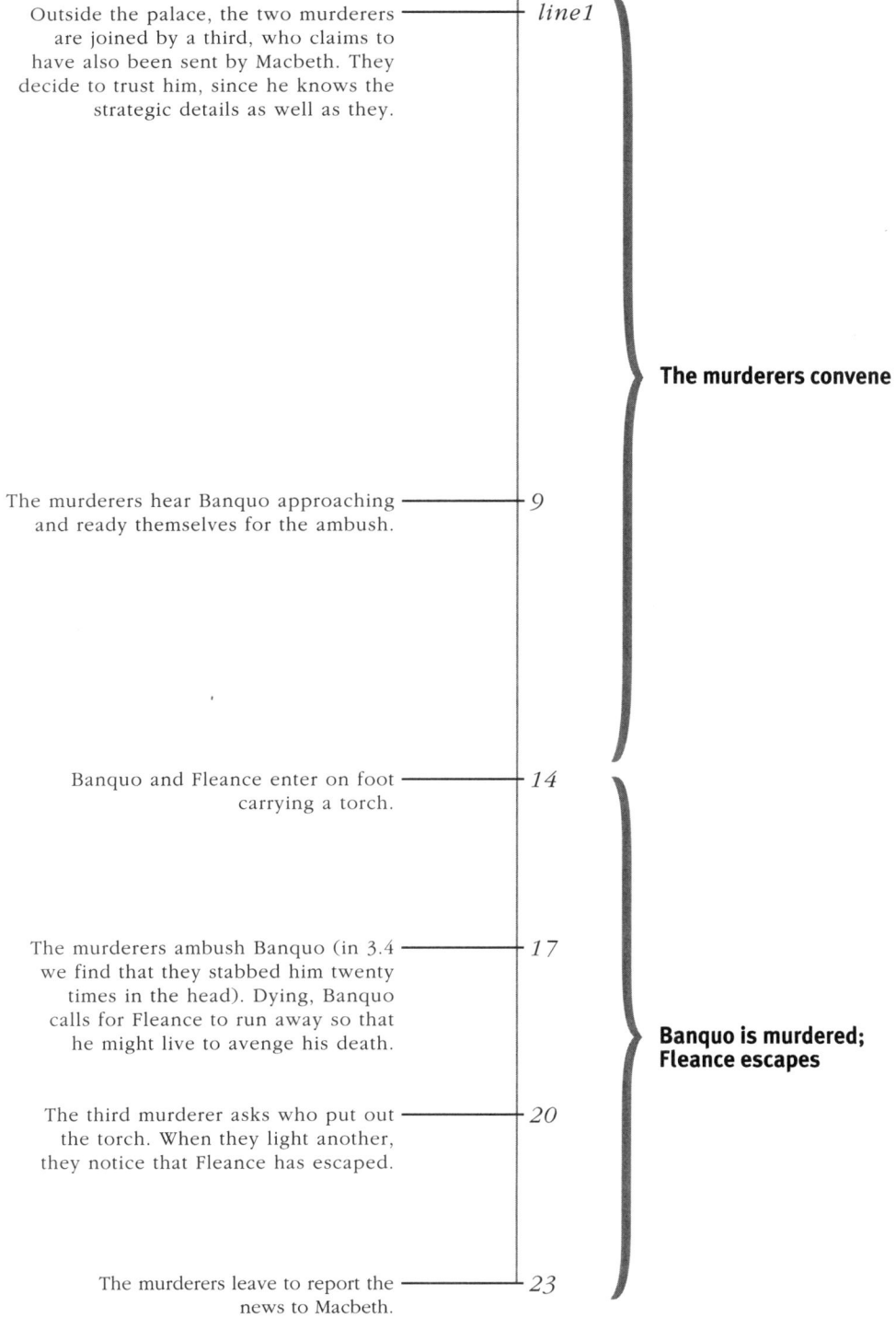

Outside the palace, the two murderers are joined by a third, who claims to have also been sent by Macbeth. They decide to trust him, since he knows the strategic details as well as they. — *line 1*

The murderers convene

The murderers hear Banquo approaching and ready themselves for the ambush. — 9

Banquo and Fleance enter on foot carrying a torch. — 14

The murderers ambush Banquo (in 3.4 we find that they stabbed him twenty times in the head). Dying, Banquo calls for Fleance to run away so that he might live to avenge his death. — 17

Banquo is murdered; Fleance escapes

The third murderer asks who put out the torch. When they light another, they notice that Fleance has escaped. — 20

The murderers leave to report the news to Macbeth. — 23

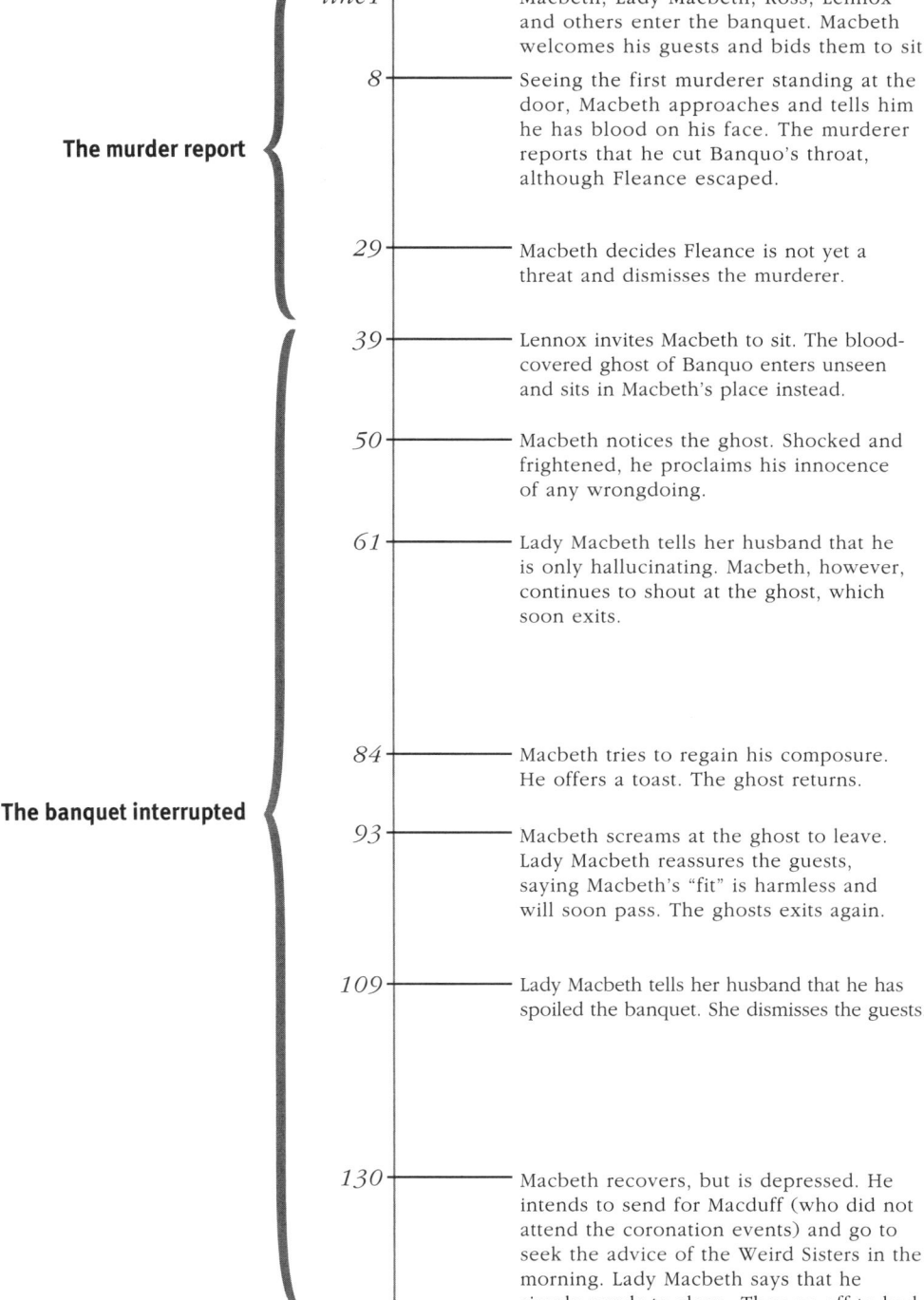

On the heath, Hecate meets the three —— *line 1*
Weird Sisters. She tells the sisters she is
angry at them for not being included in
their dealings with Macbeth.

Hecate believes that Macbeth is —— *10*
undeserving of their assistance because
he only loves himself. She demands the
Weird Sisters meet her in the morning
before their meeting with Macbeth.

Hecate instructs them to bring their —— *18*
cauldrons and spells. Hecate says she
will construct a dismal end for
Macbeth: she will conjure lying spirits
to give him a feeling of invulnerability.

**Hecate plots
Macbeth's demise**

Hecate hears her familiar calling and —— *34*
departs. The Weird Sisters hurry to
their tasks.

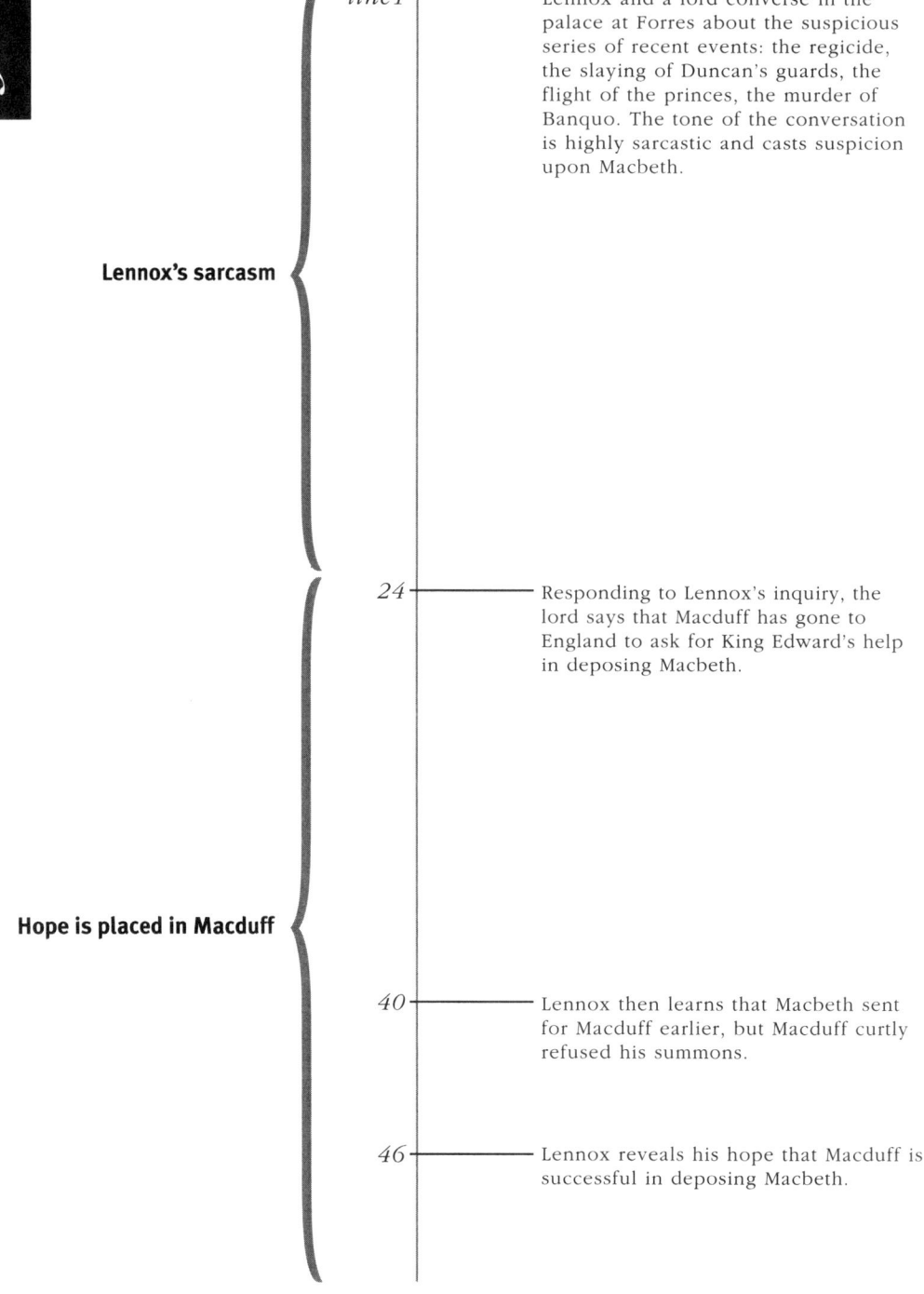

4.1

The Weird Sisters gather and await Macbeth. They dance around the cauldron and stew animal parts to concoct their spell. — *line 1*

Hecate enters with a dark entourage of three other witches. She commends the Weird Sisters for their work, leads the witches in a dance and then exits with her entourage. — *39*

} **The Weird Sisters' spell**

Macbeth enters and demands the sisters show him more of his fate. — *48*

The sisters conjure up apparitions. First, a head in armor tells Macbeth to beware of Macduff, the Thane of Fife. — *69*

The second apparition appears: a bloody child who tells Macbeth to fear no man born of woman. — *77*

The third apparition appears: a crowned child holding a tree, who tells Macbeth he will not be defeated until Birnam Forest marches to Dunsinane against him. — *90*

Macbeth asks the sisters if Banquo's sons will reign in Scotland. They respond by conjuring a procession of eight kings, followed by the ghost of Banquo. — *101*

} **The four apparitions**

The sisters dance and then vanish — *124*

Lennox enters with the news of Macduff's flight to England. — *135*

Macbeth is enraged and vows to kill Macduff's wife, children and all in his household. — *145*

} **Macbeth's rage**

DRAMATIC MAPS | 3.6 & 4.1 | 171

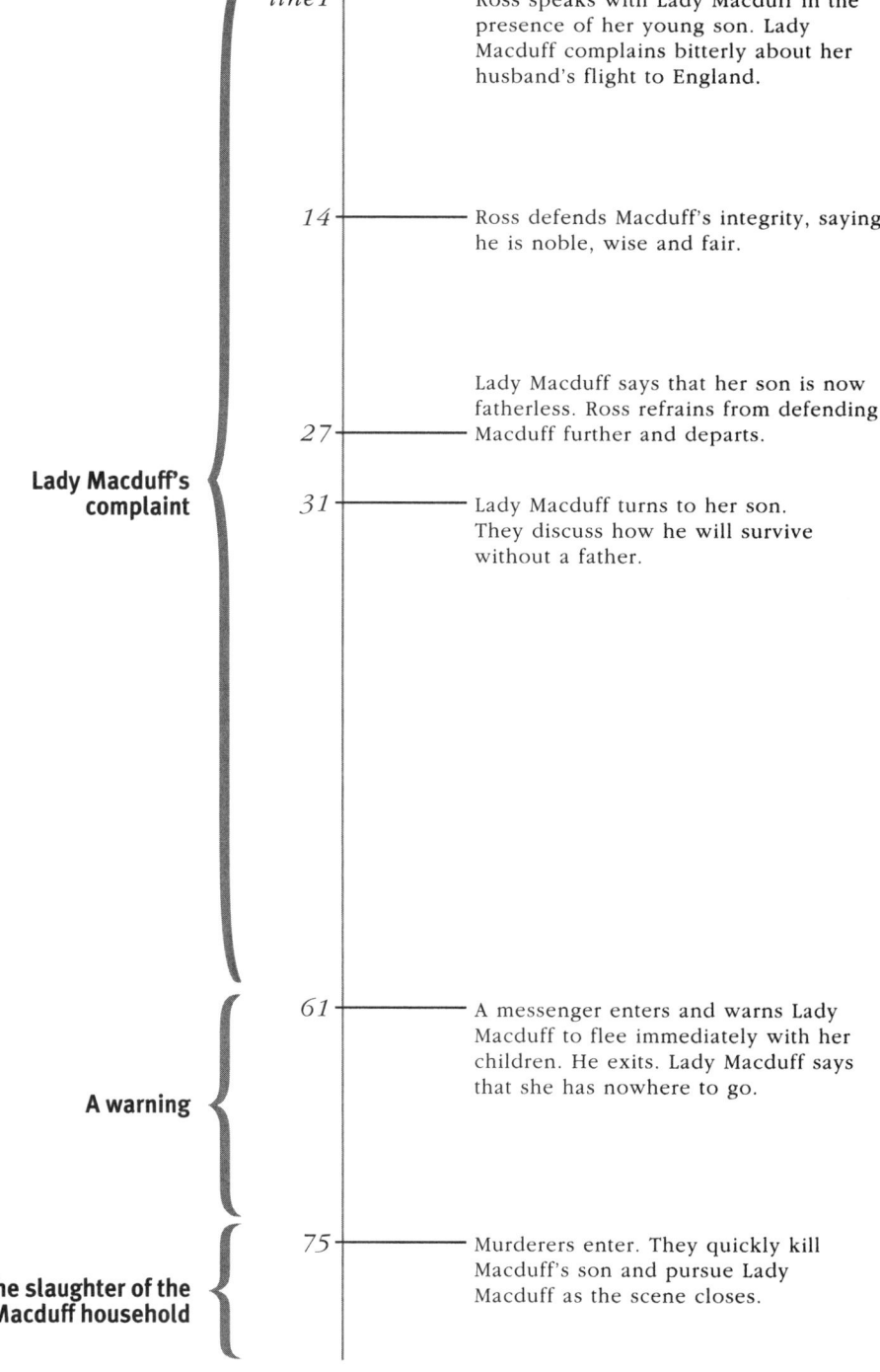

4.3

Line	Event	Section
line 1	Malcolm and Macduff ride near the palace of King Edward.	**Malcolm tests Macduff**
14	Malcolm suggests that Macduff could betray him to Macbeth, but Macduff says that he is not treacherous..	
44	Malcolm tells Macduff that England has offered him an army against Macbeth.	
51	Testing Macduff, Malcolm claims that Scotland will suffer more under his reign because of his many vices, including lust, greed and a thirst to destroy peace throughout the earth.	
104	Macduff bewails Scotland's fate, saying Malcolm is unfit to live, let alone rule.	
116	Malcolm reveals that he was only testing Macduff's loyalty to Scotland.	
142	A doctor enters. He says that King Edward is coming to cure hopelessly sick people who wait for his miraculous healing touch. The doctor exits.	**The goodness of King Edward**
162	Ross enters and tells them Macbeth is battling uprisings against his tyranny in Scotland.	**News from Scotland**
206	Ross reluctantly delivers the news that Macduff's family has been murdered.	
234	Malcolm tells Macduff to turn his grief into anger and Macduff agrees. They go to meet with King Edward.	

5.1

Lady Macbeth sleepwalks

- *line 1* — A gentlewoman who waits on Lady Macbeth tells a doctor that the queen has been sleepwalking.

- *9* — The doctor asks what the queen says during these episodes, but the gentlewoman refuses to repeat it.

- *16* — Lady Macbeth enters with a candle. The gentlewoman says the queen demands a light be always near her.

- *23* — The doctor notes that the queen rubs her hands. The gentlewoman responds that she often pretends to wash them in her sleep.

- *30* — Lady Macbeth talks in her sleep in disjointed, incriminating sentences about the murders.

- *39* — The doctor tells the gentlewoman it is wrong for her to hear these things. She replies that it is wrong for the queen to say these things.

- *42* — Lady Macbeth continues her speech, saying the smell of blood can never be removed.

- *58* — The queen exits. The doctor tells the woman this illness is beyond his skill. He says he is amazed, but won't dare speak of it.

5.2

Menteith, Angus, Caithness and Lennox hear the drums of the approaching English army, led by Prince Malcolm. — line 1

Angus says they will meet up with the army at Birnam Forest. — 5

Caithness informs them that Macbeth is busy fortifying Dunsinane. — 12

The thanes desert Macbeth

Angus says that those Macbeth commands obey only out of duty and not out of love. — 19

The thanes ride toward Birnam Forest to join Malcolm's army. — 31

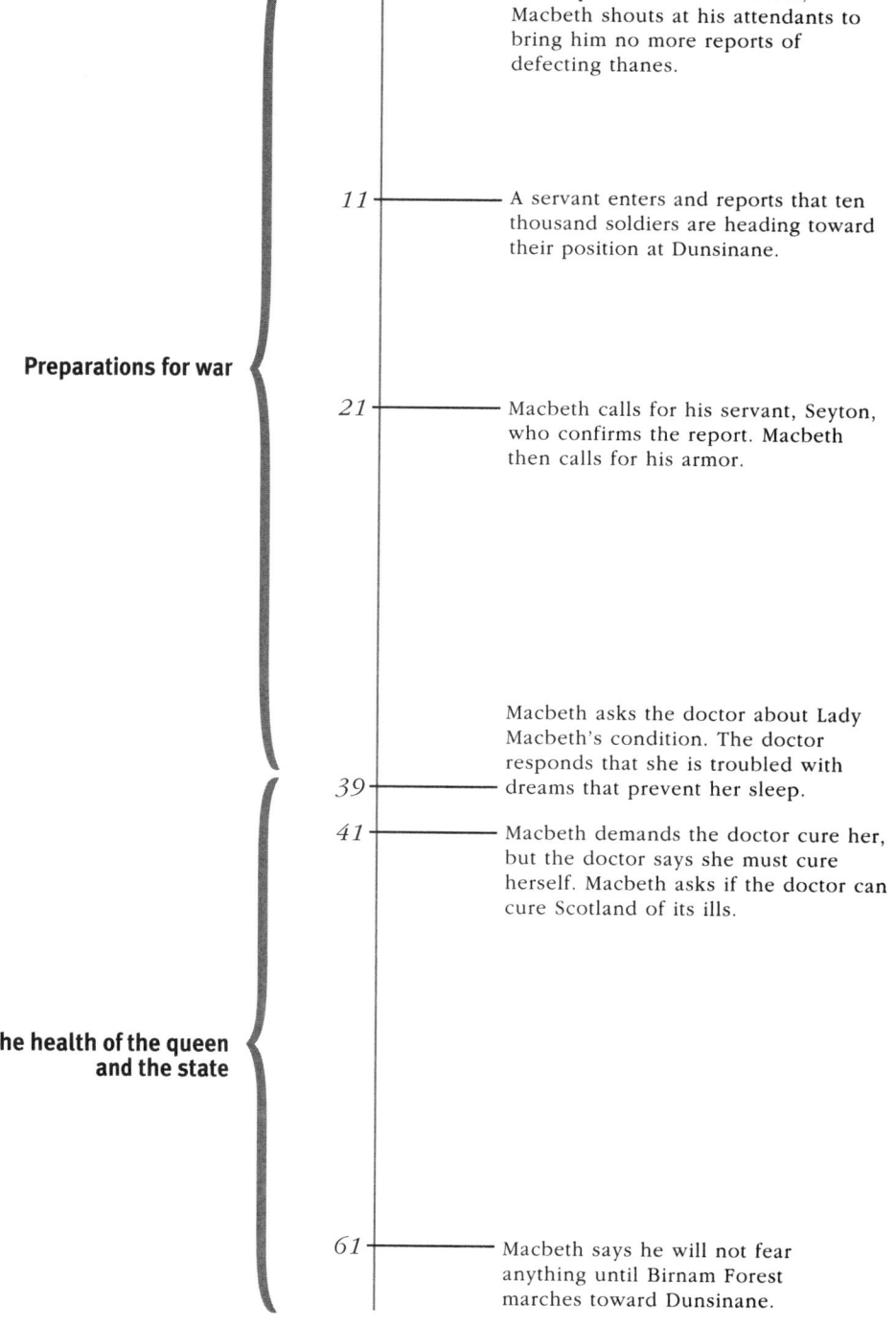

5.4

Malcolm, the thanes and the English army approach Birnam Forest.	*line 1*
Malcolm orders branches cut to conceal their numbers from Macbeth's scouts.	4
Siward reports that Macbeth has fortified Dunsinane and waits for their advance.	8
	The third apparition fulfilled
Macduff warns against underestimating Macbeth.	14
Siward urges them on toward war.	16

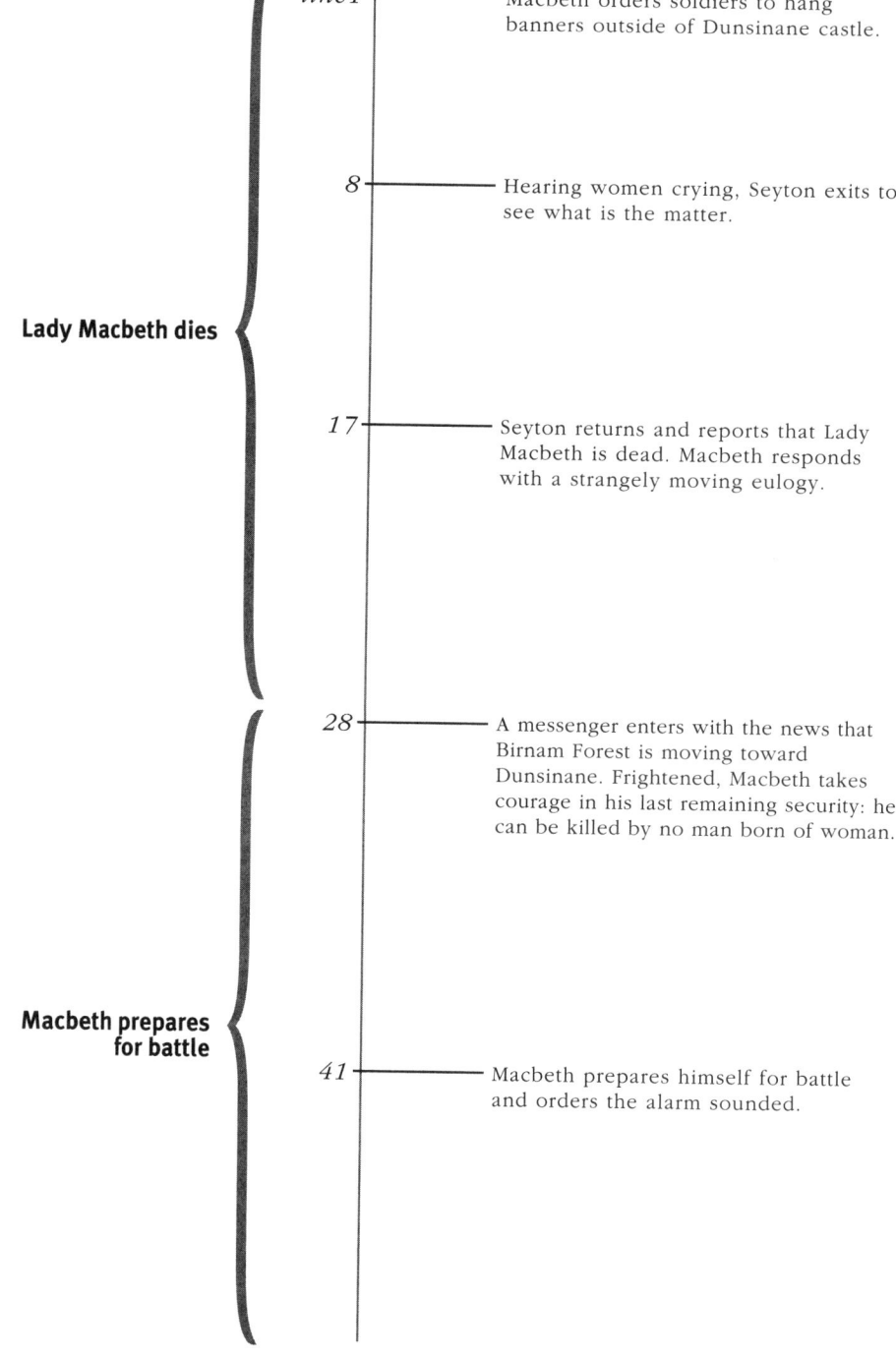

5.6

Outside Dunsinane, Malcolm orders the branches thrown down. — line 1

He directs Siward and his son to lead the assault against the castle while he and Macduff take an alternate course. — 2

The battle begins

Macduff orders the battle trumpets to sound. — 10

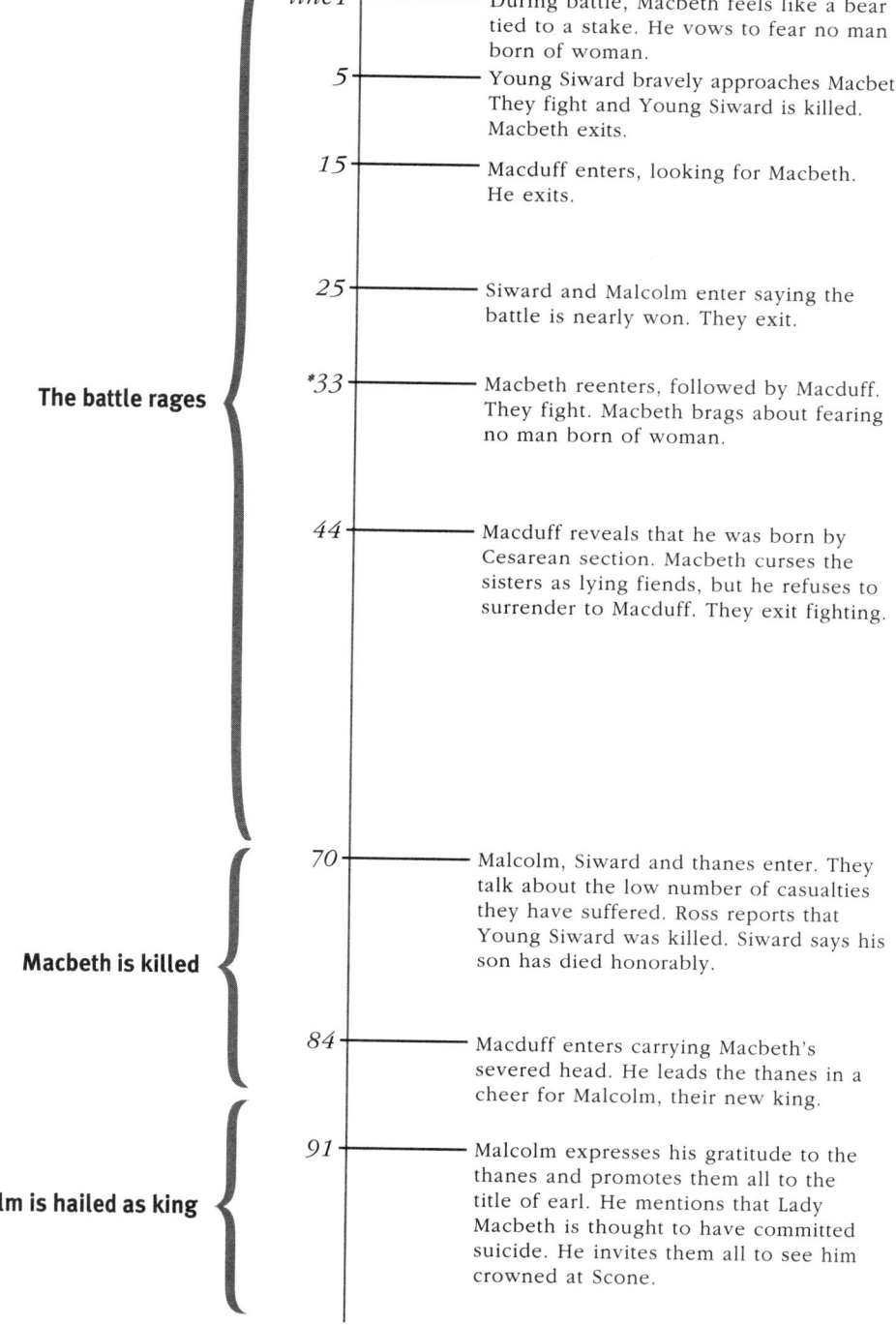

APPENDIX B: BACKGROUND

After careful thought we decided to place the background material—generally the first information you see—at the end of the guidebook. The two most compelling reasons for doing so were, first, we did not want to lose the powerful beginning of the opening chapter ("This is Macbeth"); and, second, it has been our experience that the background material is usually passed over and then read last anyway. Having said this, we feel that the material in Appendix B is extremely useful to the reader wishing an expanded view of Shakespeare's life as well as sources and nuance relating to *Macbeth*.

Shakespeare achieved success in his lifetime.

BUSINESSMAN. Born in 1564—the same year as Galileo—by the time William Shakespeare was 28, he had settled in London as an actor. At 30, he became a shareholder in the Lord Chamberlain's Men, a successful company who often staged plays at court for Queen Elizabeth I.

ACTOR. Shakespeare began as a player and part-time playwright, later focusing all of his energies on writing. He mostly acted character parts—not leading roles—although he is known to have played the character of Old Hamlet's ghost. He received far more income from his acting than from his writing royalties.

PLAYWRIGHT. He is widely regarded as the greatest dramatist of western literature and by some as the greatest thinker. Shakespeare's plays, replete with insights into human character, are performed more often than any other playwright's in history. He achieved success in his own lifetime and, by the time his wife died in 1623, a monument to Shakespeare had been erected in Holy Trinity Church in their hometown of Stratford.

1. The murder details: King Duff, 967 A.D.

According to Holinshed's *Chronicles,* King Duff, finding some of his nobles guilty of witchcraft, has them killed. This angers one nobleman, Donwald, who lost some kinsmen in this action. Donwald and his ambitious wife have King Duff as a guest in their castle. The wife drugs the king's two servants with drink and Donwald slits the king's throat. Donwald acts horrified when the murder is discovered and responds by killing the king's servants. His zeal in apprehending the murderers arouses some suspicion in the other lords, but fearing his power, they fail to act. The sun and moon are not seen for six months after the regicide.

2. The overall story: King Duncan, 1040 A.D.

Duncan is King of Strathclyde, a region in western Scotland. Eventually, he ascends the throne of Scotland and his cousin, King Macbeth of Moray, serves him as a general. The battles against Macdonwald and Sweno are included, but the English King Canute is also defeated and required to pay an enormous sum at St. Colme's Inch. Duncan is known as a kindly but weak king whose thanes (or lords) fight his battles for him. Following one such battle, Macbeth meets three woman who prophesy his future. With his wife's encouragement and the help of Banquo, Macbeth murders King Duncan and assumes the throne of Scotland. The princes flee to England and Ireland. Macbeth reigns with integrity for seventeen years. During the last seven years of his reign, however, Macbeth begins to fear for his life and he murders many nobles. He first arranges for the murders of Banquo and his son, Fleance. Fleance escapes to later found the Stuart Dynasty from which King James is born. Macbeth hears the second set of equivocal prophecies from wizards and witches. Malcolm's army attacks Macbeth at Dunsinane and Macduff beheads him after revealing he was born by Cesarean section. Malcolm becomes king and names the thanes Scotland's first earls. Also included are the slaughter of the Macduff household, Macduff's plea to Malcolm and Malcolm's subsequent testing of Macduff.

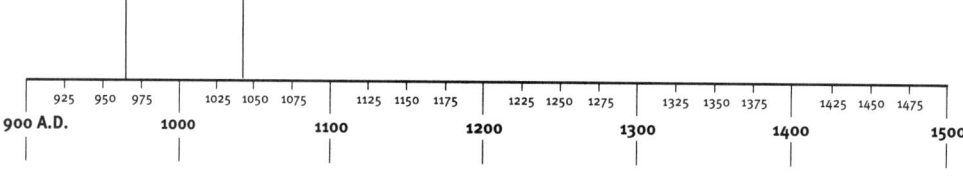

Macbeth is a blend of two historical accounts.

RAPHAEL HOLINSHED, *CHRONICLES*, 1587

Holinshed's *Chronicles of England, Scotland and Ireland* was first published in 1577. Ten years later, a posthumous, revised edition was published, missing several passages ordered removed by Queen Elizabeth. This 1587 edition is likely Shakespeare's source for *Macbeth*.

Holinshed provides the overall story for the Shakespearean tragedy with little variance: Duncan, Macbeth, Lady Macbeth, Banquo, Fleance, Malcolm, Macduff, Siward and the Weird Sisters remain well intact. The major departure of Shakespeare's drama from his source are the actual details of the regicide. Shakespeare blended events from the murder of King Duff—some 70 years before Macbeth— into the murder of Duncan. Details from the murder of King Duff, such as the king's post-battle celebration, his overnight stay at the murderer's castle, the ambitious wife, the drugging of the guards and their subsequent murder for the crime, provided Shakespeare with a more interesting account than the murder of King Duncan. The Duff account also solved Shakespeare's problem of Banquo's culpability. According to Holinshed, Banquo, thought to be an ancestor to King James, assisted Macbeth in the murder of Duncan. Shakespeare's use of the Duff details eliminated his need to include an accomplice.

1040 Macbeth murders Duncan
In a conspiracy with his ambitious wife and some friends, Macbeth kills Duncan and becomes king himself. He rules Scotland for seventeen years: ten as an honorable king and seven as a paranoid tyrant.

1057 Malcolm avenges his father's murder
Malcolm returns to Scotland and, aided by the English, finally avenges his father's murder. He reigns as Malcolm III and dies in 1093 of natural causes. His marriage to the English princess, Margaret, begins a period of Scottish Anglicization.

1292 Scotland becomes a vassal state of England
When the infant Queen Margaret dies, no fewer than thirteen descendants make claims to the throne. Proclaiming suzerainty (one nation claiming rulership over another's affairs), Edward I of England names John de Baliol (great-grandson of Malcolm III) King of Scotland.

1297 William Wallace leads Scottish uprising
Struggling against English rule, Wallace and his soldiers overcome English forces and, acting under Baliol, reinstate Scottish rule.

1488 Scotland unified
James IV ends the revolt of the nobility in Scotland, thus unifying his country. In true renaissance form, James is a patron of the arts and education. In 1503 he marries Margaret Tudor, a move which will eventually lead to the rule of England and Scotland under a single crown.

1567 Mary, Queen of Scots forced to abdicate
Mary, a leader in the Counter Reformation movement in Scotland and later England, is defeated in civil war. As a result, she is forced to abdicate her throne to her one-year-old son, James VI.

1603 James VI becomes King of England
After completing a military alliance with Elizabeth I of England late in the sixteenth century, James refuses to intervene when she has his mother executed. He inherits the crown of England on Elizabeth's death.

1606 Shakespeare's *Macbeth* is written

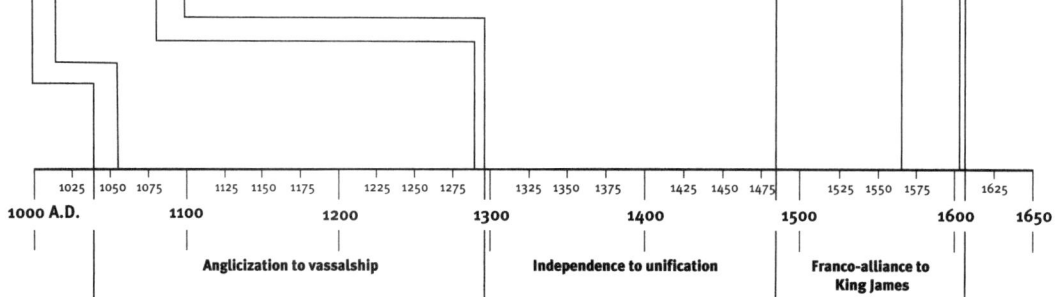

Anglicization to vassalship | Independence to unification | Franco-alliance to King James

The movement toward a single ruler over England and Scotland.

HISTORICAL TRAJECTORY. At the time of Shakespeare's first performance of *Macbeth,* Scotland's history could be viewed as a movement from self-rule, through vassalship, independence and civil strife, ending in the unifying rule of James VI (James I to the English). Shakespeare's challenge was to find a prudent point in Scotland's history that would downplay Scotland's struggle for independence and civil unrest.

The historic figure of Macbeth was a brilliant choice. Historically, his murder of Duncan forced Prince Malcolm's flight to England. While in England, Malcolm married the English Princess Margaret, who was eventually to replace the Celtic religious practices of Scotland with those of her homeland, leading the way for the Anglicization of Scotland. Shakespeare thus portrayed Macbeth as an abhorrent protagonist and Malcolm as a redeemer of Scotland, as well as an ambassador of good relations between his country and England.

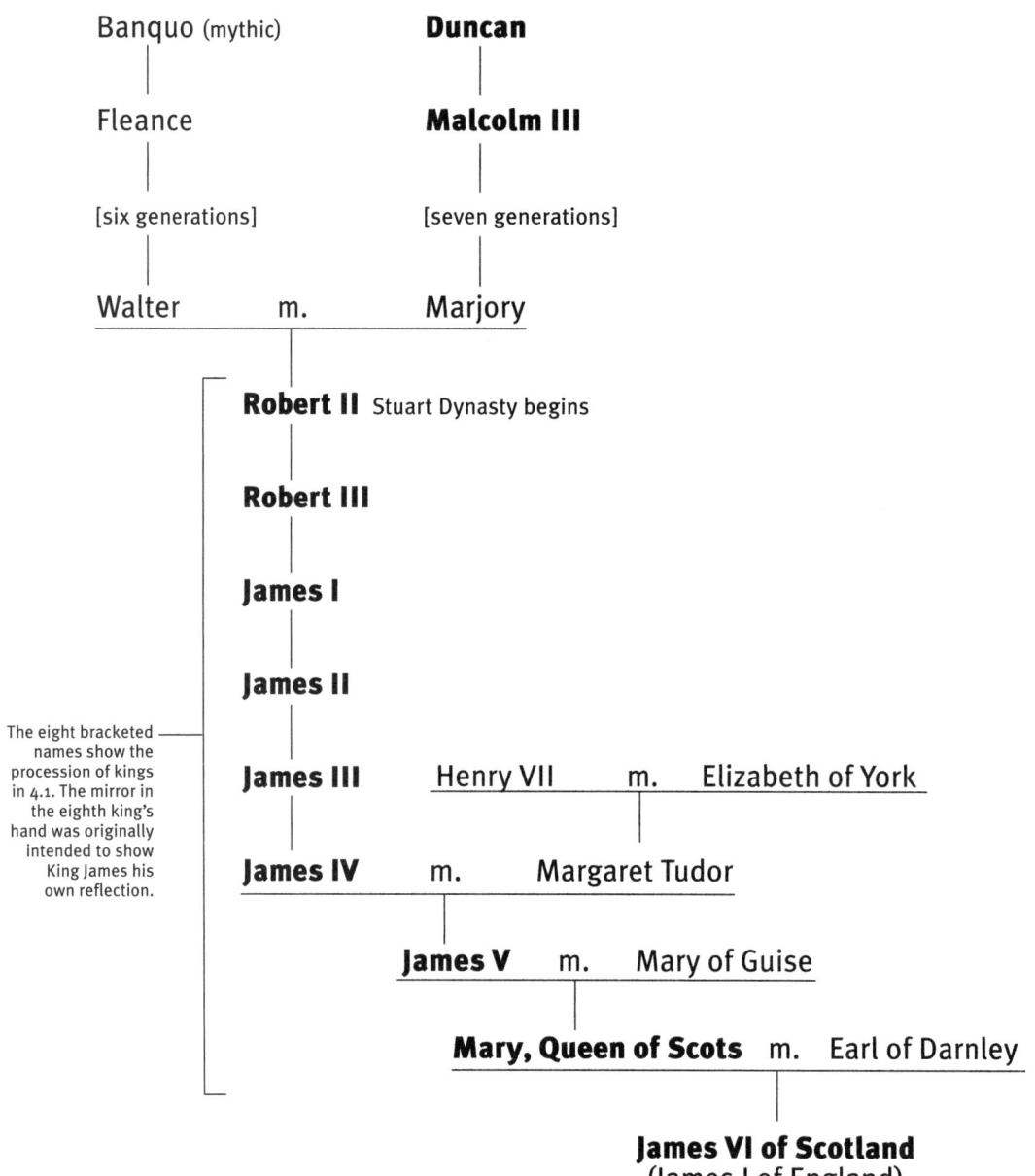

Shakespeare, James and the Holinshed procession of kings.

ALL THE KING'S MEN. Holinshed, in his *Chronicles of England, Scotland and Ireland,* lists eight majesties in the genealogy from Banquo to King James VI (a woman—Mary, Queen of Scots—is the eighth). In 4.1, Shakespeare has Macbeth ask the Weird Sisters whether Banquo's sons will truly sit on the throne of Scotland. In reply, the sisters conjure a procession of eight kings, each holding symbols of power. Shakespeare perhaps "unsexed" Mary in his dramatic rendition of the procession, so as not to emphasize the mother of his new king and patron. James chose not to intervene in his mother's execution by Queen Elizabeth, her cousin, and became King of Scotland after her death. In Shakespeare's procession, the eighth king held a mirror, presumably to show King James his own reflection.

Born June 19, 1566
Born at Edinburgh Castle, James is the only son of Mary, Queen of Scots.

Becomes King of Scotland, 1567
When Mary is forced to abdicate, the infant James becomes King James VI. Scotland is ruled by regents.

Assumes rule of Scotland, 1581
James assumes actual rule of Scotland with the help of his favorites, James Stuart and Esmé Stuart, Duke of Lennox.

Kidnapped by Protestants, 1582
James is kidnapped by a group of Protestant nobles led by William Ruthven, Earl of Gowrie. He escapes the next year.

Forms alliance with England, 1586
James forms a military alliance with Elizabeth I of England, by the Treaty of Berwick.

Authors *Daemonologie*, 1597
James writes a book about witchcraft, attempting to prove its existence and countering some skepticism generated by Scot's *The Discoverie of Witchcraft*, published in 1584, which took a more psychological stance.

Ascends the throne of England, 1603
On her deathbed, Elizabeth at last names James VI heir to the English throne. He succeeds her as James I of England and becomes patron of Shakespeare's theatrical company.

Commissions new bible translation, 1604
A confirmed Protestant, James commissions a new translation of the Bible, the *Authorized King James Version*.

Conspirators plot his assassination, 1605
A group of conspirators plot to assassinate James. Thirty-six barrels of gun powder are stored beneath the House of Lords, to be ignited by Guy Fawkes. A letter exposes the plot and the conspirators are executed.

Dies at age 60
On March 27, 1625,, James I dies in Hertfordshire, England. He is succeeded by his son, Charles I.

Macbeth: the perfect play for Shakespeare's new patron.

FIT FOR A KING. King James I became the new patron of Shakespeare's acting company. An astute businessman, Shakespeare custom-wrote *Macbeth* for his new king. Set in James' homeland of Scotland, the play's villains, the Macbeths, were guilty of the highest offense—the murder of a king (a plot to murder James had been foiled only a year prior to the first performance). The play's hero, Malcolm, paved the way for good relations with England. Banquo was portrayed, not as an accomplice to murder, but as an innocent victim whose vengeance was the establishment of the royal line from which James was said to have descended. *Macbeth* dealt with witchcraft—a subject of great interest to James, author of *Daemonology*. Lastly, although far from a morality play, *Macbeth* was infused with Christian symbolism—again, a subject of great interest to the man who authorized a new translation of the bible.